Mometrix
TEST PREPARATION

MTLE

Physical Education Secrets Study Guide

DEAR FUTURE EXAM SUCCESS STORY

First of all, **THANK YOU** for purchasing Mometrix study materials!

Second, congratulations! You are one of the few determined test-takers who are committed to doing whatever it takes to excel on your exam. **You have come to the right place.** We developed these study materials with one goal in mind: to deliver you the information you need in a format that's concise and easy to use.

In addition to optimizing your guide for the content of the test, we've outlined our recommended steps for breaking down the preparation process into small, attainable goals so you can make sure you stay on track.

We've also analyzed the entire test-taking process, identifying the most common pitfalls and showing how you can overcome them and be ready for any curveball the test throws you.

Standardized testing is one of the biggest obstacles on your road to success, which only increases the importance of doing well in the high-pressure, high-stakes environment of test day. Your results on this test could have a significant impact on your future, and this guide provides the information and practical advice to help you achieve your full potential on test day.

Your success is our success

We would love to hear from you! If you would like to share the story of your exam success or if you have any questions or comments in regard to our products, please contact us at **800-673-8175** or **support@mometrix.com**.

Thanks again for your business and we wish you continued success!

Sincerely,
The Mometrix Test Preparation Team

Need more help? Check out our flashcards at:
http://mometrixflashcards.com/MTLE

Written and edited by the Mometrix Exam Secrets Test Prep Team
Printed in the United States of America

TABLE OF CONTENTS

Introduction

Thank you for purchasing this resource! You have made the choice to prepare yourself for a test that could have a huge impact on your future, and this guide is designed to help you be fully ready for test day. Obviously, it's important to have a solid understanding of the test material, but you also need to be prepared for the unique environment and stressors of the test, so that you can perform to the best of your abilities.

For this purpose, the first section that appears in this guide is the **Secret Keys**. We've devoted countless hours to meticulously researching what works and what doesn't, and we've boiled down our findings to the five most impactful steps you can take to improve your performance on the test. We start at the beginning with study planning and move through the preparation process, all the way to the testing strategies that will help you get the most out of what you know when you're finally sitting in front of the test.

We recommend that you start preparing for your test as far in advance as possible. However, if you've bought this guide as a last-minute study resource and only have a few days before your test, we recommend that you skip over the first two Secret Keys since they address a long-term study plan.

If you struggle with **test anxiety**, we strongly encourage you to check out our recommendations for how you can overcome it. Test anxiety is a formidable foe, but it can be beaten, and we want to make sure you have the tools you need to defeat it.

Secret Key #1 – Plan Big, Study Small

There's a lot riding on your performance. If you want to ace this test, you're going to need to keep your skills sharp and the material fresh in your mind. You need a plan that lets you review everything you need to know while still fitting in your schedule. We'll break this strategy down into three categories.

Information Organization

Start with the information you already have: the official test outline. From this, you can make a complete list of all the concepts you need to cover before the test. Organize these concepts into groups that can be studied together, and create a list of any related vocabulary you need to learn so you can brush up on any difficult terms. You'll want to keep this vocabulary list handy once you actually start studying since you may need to add to it along the way.

Time Management

Once you have your set of study concepts, decide how to spread them out over the time you have left before the test. Break your study plan into small, clear goals so you have a manageable task for each day and know exactly what you're doing. Then just focus on one small step at a time. When you manage your time this way, you don't need to spend hours at a time studying. Studying a small block of content for a short period each day helps you retain information better and avoid stressing over how much you have left to do. You can relax knowing that you have a plan to cover everything in time. In order for this strategy to be effective though, you have to start studying early and stick to your schedule. Avoid the exhaustion and futility that comes from last-minute cramming!

Study Environment

The environment you study in has a big impact on your learning. Studying in a coffee shop, while probably more enjoyable, is not likely to be as fruitful as studying in a quiet room. It's important to keep distractions to a minimum. You're only planning to study for a short block of time, so make the most of it. Don't pause to check your phone or get up to find a snack. It's also important to **avoid multitasking**. Research has consistently shown that multitasking will make your studying dramatically less effective. Your study area should also be comfortable and well-lit so you don't have the distraction of straining your eyes or sitting on an uncomfortable chair.

The time of day you study is also important. You want to be rested and alert. Don't wait until just before bedtime. Study when you'll be most likely to comprehend and remember. Even better, if you know what time of day your test will be, set that time aside for study. That way your brain will be used to working on that subject at that specific time and you'll have a better chance of recalling information.

Finally, it can be helpful to team up with others who are studying for the same test. Your actual studying should be done in as isolated an environment as possible, but the work of organizing the information and setting up the study plan can be divided up. In between study sessions, you can discuss with your teammates the concepts that you're all studying and quiz each other on the details. Just be sure that your teammates are as serious about the test as you are. If you find that your study time is being replaced with social time, you might need to find a new team.

Secret Key #2 – Make Your Studying Count

You're devoting a lot of time and effort to preparing for this test, so you want to be absolutely certain it will pay off. This means doing more than just reading the content and hoping you can remember it on test day. It's important to make every minute of study count. There are two main areas you can focus on to make your studying count.

Retention

It doesn't matter how much time you study if you can't remember the material. You need to make sure you are retaining the concepts. To check your retention of the information you're learning, try recalling it at later times with minimal prompting. Try carrying around flashcards and glance at one or two from time to time or ask a friend who's also studying for the test to quiz you.

To enhance your retention, look for ways to put the information into practice so that you can apply it rather than simply recalling it. If you're using the information in practical ways, it will be much easier to remember. Similarly, it helps to solidify a concept in your mind if you're not only reading it to yourself but also explaining it to someone else. Ask a friend to let you teach them about a concept you're a little shaky on (or speak aloud to an imaginary audience if necessary). As you try to summarize, define, give examples, and answer your friend's questions, you'll understand the concepts better and they will stay with you longer. Finally, step back for a big picture view and ask yourself how each piece of information fits with the whole subject. When you link the different concepts together and see them working together as a whole, it's easier to remember the individual components.

Finally, practice showing your work on any multi-step problems, even if you're just studying. Writing out each step you take to solve a problem will help solidify the process in your mind, and you'll be more likely to remember it during the test.

Modality

Modality simply refers to the means or method by which you study. Choosing a study modality that fits your own individual learning style is crucial. No two people learn best in exactly the same way, so it's important to know your strengths and use them to your advantage.

For example, if you learn best by visualization, focus on visualizing a concept in your mind and draw an image or a diagram. Try color-coding your notes, illustrating them, or creating symbols that will trigger your mind to recall a learned concept. If you learn best by hearing or discussing information, find a study partner who learns the same way or read aloud to yourself. Think about how to put the information in your own words. Imagine that you are giving a lecture on the topic and record yourself so you can listen to it later.

For any learning style, flashcards can be helpful. Organize the information so you can take advantage of spare moments to review. Underline key words or phrases. Use different colors for different categories. Mnemonic devices (such as creating a short list in which every item starts with the same letter) can also help with retention. Find what works best for you and use it to store the information in your mind most effectively and easily.

Secret Key #3 – Practice the Right Way

Your success on test day depends not only on how many hours you put into preparing, but also on whether you prepared the right way. It's good to check along the way to see if your studying is paying off. One of the most effective ways to do this is by taking practice tests to evaluate your progress. Practice tests are useful because they show exactly where you need to improve. Every time you take a practice test, pay special attention to these three groups of questions:

- The questions you got wrong
- The questions you had to guess on, even if you guessed right
- The questions you found difficult or slow to work through

This will show you exactly what your weak areas are, and where you need to devote more study time. Ask yourself why each of these questions gave you trouble. Was it because you didn't understand the material? Was it because you didn't remember the vocabulary? Do you need more repetitions on this type of question to build speed and confidence? Dig into those questions and figure out how you can strengthen your weak areas as you go back to review the material.

Additionally, many practice tests have a section explaining the answer choices. It can be tempting to read the explanation and think that you now have a good understanding of the concept. However, an explanation likely only covers part of the question's broader context. Even if the explanation makes perfect sense, **go back and investigate** every concept related to the question until you're positive you have a thorough understanding.

As you go along, keep in mind that the practice test is just that: practice. Memorizing these questions and answers will not be very helpful on the actual test because it is unlikely to have any of the same exact questions. If you only know the right answers to the sample questions, you won't be prepared for the real thing. **Study the concepts** until you understand them fully, and then you'll be able to answer any question that shows up on the test.

It's important to wait on the practice tests until you're ready. If you take a test on your first day of study, you may be overwhelmed by the amount of material covered and how much you need to learn. Work up to it gradually.

On test day, you'll need to be prepared for answering questions, managing your time, and using the test-taking strategies you've learned. It's a lot to balance, like a mental marathon that will have a big impact on your future. Like training for a marathon, you'll need to start slowly and work your way up. When test day arrives, you'll be ready.

Start with the strategies you've read in the first two Secret Keys—plan your course and study in the way that works best for you. If you have time, consider using multiple study resources to get different approaches to the same concepts. It can be helpful to see difficult concepts from more than one angle. Then find a good source for practice tests. Many times, the test website will suggest potential study resources or provide sample tests.

Practice Test Strategy

If you're able to find at least three practice tests, we recommend this strategy:

Untimed and Open-Book Practice

Take the first test with no time constraints and with your notes and study guide handy. Take your time and focus on applying the strategies you've learned.

Timed and Open-Book Practice

Take the second practice test open-book as well, but set a timer and practice pacing yourself to finish in time.

Timed and Closed-Book Practice

Take any other practice tests as if it were test day. Set a timer and put away your study materials. Sit at a table or desk in a quiet room, imagine yourself at the testing center, and answer questions as quickly and accurately as possible.

Keep repeating timed and closed-book tests on a regular basis until you run out of practice tests or it's time for the actual test. Your mind will be ready for the schedule and stress of test day, and you'll be able to focus on recalling the material you've learned.

Secret Key #4 – Pace Yourself

Once you're fully prepared for the material on the test, your biggest challenge on test day will be managing your time. Just knowing that the clock is ticking can make you panic even if you have plenty of time left. Work on pacing yourself so you can build confidence against the time constraints of the exam. Pacing is a difficult skill to master, especially in a high-pressure environment, so **practice is vital**.

Set time expectations for your pace based on how much time is available. For example, if a section has 60 questions and the time limit is 30 minutes, you know you have to average 30 seconds or less per question in order to answer them all. Although 30 seconds is the hard limit, set 25 seconds per question as your goal, so you reserve extra time to spend on harder questions. When you budget extra time for the harder questions, you no longer have any reason to stress when those questions take longer to answer.

Don't let this time expectation distract you from working through the test at a calm, steady pace, but keep it in mind so you don't spend too much time on any one question. Recognize that taking extra time on one question you don't understand may keep you from answering two that you do understand later in the test. If your time limit for a question is up and you're still not sure of the answer, mark it and move on, and come back to it later if the time and the test format allow. If the testing format doesn't allow you to return to earlier questions, just make an educated guess; then put it out of your mind and move on.

On the easier questions, be careful not to rush. It may seem wise to hurry through them so you have more time for the challenging ones, but it's not worth missing one if you know the concept and just didn't take the time to read the question fully. Work efficiently but make sure you understand the question and have looked at all of the answer choices, since more than one may seem right at first.

Even if you're paying attention to the time, you may find yourself a little behind at some point. You should speed up to get back on track, but do so wisely. Don't panic; just take a few seconds less on each question until you're caught up. Don't guess without thinking, but do look through the answer choices and eliminate any you know are wrong. If you can get down to two choices, it is often worthwhile to guess from those. Once you've chosen an answer, move on and don't dwell on any that you skipped or had to hurry through. If a question was taking too long, chances are it was one of the harder ones, so you weren't as likely to get it right anyway.

On the other hand, if you find yourself getting ahead of schedule, it may be beneficial to slow down a little. The more quickly you work, the more likely you are to make a careless mistake that will affect your score. You've budgeted time for each question, so don't be afraid to spend that time. Practice an efficient but careful pace to get the most out of the time you have.

Secret Key #5 – Have a Plan for Guessing

When you're taking the test, you may find yourself stuck on a question. Some of the answer choices seem better than others, but you don't see the one answer choice that is obviously correct. What do you do?

The scenario described above is very common, yet most test takers have not effectively prepared for it. Developing and practicing a plan for guessing may be one of the single most effective uses of your time as you get ready for the exam.

In developing your plan for guessing, there are three questions to address:

- When should you start the guessing process?
- How should you narrow down the choices?
- Which answer should you choose?

When to Start the Guessing Process

Unless your plan for guessing is to select C every time (which, despite its merits, is not what we recommend), you need to leave yourself enough time to apply your answer elimination strategies. Since you have a limited amount of time for each question, that means that if you're going to give yourself the best shot at guessing correctly, you have to decide quickly whether or not you will guess.

Of course, the best-case scenario is that you don't have to guess at all, so first, see if you can answer the question based on your knowledge of the subject and basic reasoning skills. Focus on the key words in the question and try to jog your memory of related topics. Give yourself a chance to bring the knowledge to mind, but once you realize that you don't have (or you can't access) the knowledge you need to answer the question, it's time to start the guessing process.

It's almost always better to start the guessing process too early than too late. It only takes a few seconds to remember something and answer the question from knowledge. Carefully eliminating wrong answer choices takes longer. Plus, going through the process of eliminating answer choices can actually help jog your memory.

Summary: Start the guessing process as soon as you decide that you can't answer the question based on your knowledge.

How to Narrow Down the Choices

The next chapter in this book (**Test-Taking Strategies**) includes a wide range of strategies for how to approach questions and how to look for answer choices to eliminate. You will definitely want to read those carefully, practice them, and figure out which ones work best for you. Here though, we're going to address a mindset rather than a particular strategy.

Your odds of guessing an answer correctly depend on how many options you are choosing from.

Number of options left	5	4	3	2	1
Odds of guessing correctly	20%	25%	33%	50%	100%

You can see from this chart just how valuable it is to be able to eliminate incorrect answers and make an educated guess, but there are two things that many test takers do that cause them to miss out on the benefits of guessing:

- Accidentally eliminating the correct answer
- Selecting an answer based on an impression

We'll look at the first one here, and the second one in the next section.

To avoid accidentally eliminating the correct answer, we recommend a thought exercise called **the $5 challenge**. In this challenge, you only eliminate an answer choice from contention if you are willing to bet $5 on it being wrong. Why $5? Five dollars is a small but not insignificant amount of money. It's an amount you could afford to lose but wouldn't want to throw away. And while losing $5 once might not hurt too much, doing it twenty times will set you back $100. In the same way, each small decision you make—eliminating a choice here, guessing on a question there—won't by itself impact your score very much, but when you put them all together, they can make a big difference. By holding each answer choice elimination decision to a higher standard, you can reduce the risk of accidentally eliminating the correct answer.

The $5 challenge can also be applied in a positive sense: If you are willing to bet $5 that an answer choice *is* correct, go ahead and mark it as correct.

Summary: Only eliminate an answer choice if you are willing to bet $5 that it is wrong.

Which Answer to Choose

You're taking the test. You've run into a hard question and decided you'll have to guess. You've eliminated all the answer choices you're willing to bet $5 on. Now you have to pick an answer. Why do we even need to talk about this? Why can't you just pick whichever one you feel like when the time comes?

The answer to these questions is that if you don't come into the test with a plan, you'll rely on your impression to select an answer choice, and if you do that, you risk falling into a trap. The test writers know that everyone who takes their test will be guessing on some of the questions, so they intentionally write wrong answer choices to seem plausible. You still have to pick an answer though, and if the wrong answer choices are designed to look right, how can you ever be sure that you're not falling for their trap? The best solution we've found to this dilemma is to take the decision out of your hands entirely. Here is the process we recommend:

Once you've eliminated any choices that you are confident (willing to bet $5) are wrong, select the first remaining choice as your answer.

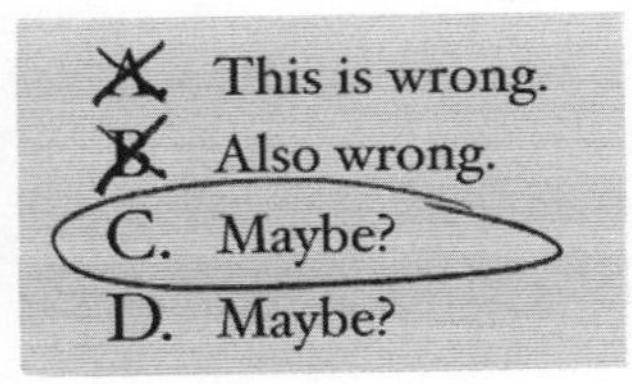

Whether you choose to select the first remaining choice, the second, or the last, the important thing is that you use some preselected standard. Using this approach guarantees that you will not be enticed into selecting an answer choice that looks right, because you are not basing your decision on how the answer choices look.

This is not meant to make you question your knowledge. Instead, it is to help you recognize the difference between your knowledge and your impressions. There's a huge difference between thinking an answer is right because of what you know, and thinking an answer is right because it looks or sounds like it should be right.

Summary: To ensure that your selection is appropriately random, make a predetermined selection from among all answer choices you have not eliminated.

Test-Taking Strategies

This section contains a list of test-taking strategies that you may find helpful as you work through the test. By taking what you know and applying logical thought, you can maximize your chances of answering any question correctly!

It is very important to realize that every question is different and every person is different: no single strategy will work on every question, and no single strategy will work for every person. That's why we've included all of them here, so you can try them out and determine which ones work best for different types of questions and which ones work best for you.

Question Strategies

READ CAREFULLY

Read the question and the answer choices carefully. Don't miss the question because you misread the terms. You have plenty of time to read each question thoroughly and make sure you understand what is being asked. Yet a happy medium must be attained, so don't waste too much time. You must read carefully and efficiently.

CONTEXTUAL CLUES

Look for contextual clues. If the question includes a word you are not familiar with, look at the immediate context for some indication of what the word might mean. Contextual clues can often give you all the information you need to decipher the meaning of an unfamiliar word. Even if you can't determine the meaning, you may be able to narrow down the possibilities enough to make a solid guess at the answer to the question.

PREFIXES

If you're having trouble with a word in the question or answer choices, try dissecting it. Take advantage of every clue that the word might include. Prefixes can be a huge help. Usually, they allow you to determine a basic meaning. *Pre-* means before, *post-* means after, *pro-* is positive, *de-* is negative. From prefixes, you can get an idea of the general meaning of the word and try to put it into context.

HEDGE WORDS

Watch out for critical hedge words, such as *likely, may, can, often, almost, mostly, usually, generally, rarely,* and *sometimes.* Question writers insert these hedge phrases to cover every possibility. Often an answer choice will be wrong simply because it leaves no room for exception. Be on guard for answer choices that have definitive words such as *exactly* and *always.*

SWITCHBACK WORDS

Stay alert for *switchbacks.* These are the words and phrases frequently used to alert you to shifts in thought. The most common switchback words are *but, although,* and *however.* Others include *nevertheless, on the other hand, even though, while, in spite of, despite,* and *regardless of.* Switchback words are important to catch because they can change the direction of the question or an answer choice.

FACE VALUE

When in doubt, use common sense. Accept the situation in the problem at face value. Don't read too much into it. These problems will not require you to make wild assumptions. If you have to go beyond creativity and warp time or space in order to have an answer choice fit the question, then you should move on and consider the other answer choices. These are normal problems rooted in reality. The applicable relationship or explanation may not be readily apparent, but it is there for you to figure out. Use your common sense to interpret anything that isn't clear.

Answer Choice Strategies

⊘ Answer Selection

The most thorough way to pick an answer choice is to identify and eliminate wrong answers until only one is left, then confirm it is the correct answer. Sometimes an answer choice may immediately seem right, but be careful. The test writers will usually put more than one reasonable answer choice on each question, so take a second to read all of them and make sure that the other choices are not equally obvious. As long as you have time left, it is better to read every answer choice than to pick the first one that looks right without checking the others.

⊘ Answer Choice Families

An answer choice family consists of two (in rare cases, three) answer choices that are very similar in construction and cannot all be true at the same time. If you see two answer choices that are direct opposites or parallels, one of them is usually the correct answer. For instance, if one answer choice says that quantity *x* increases and another either says that quantity *x* decreases (opposite) or says that quantity *y* increases (parallel), then those answer choices would fall into the same family. An answer choice that doesn't match the construction of the answer choice family is more likely to be incorrect. Most questions will not have answer choice families, but when they do appear, you should be prepared to recognize them.

⊘ Eliminate Answers

Eliminate answer choices as soon as you realize they are wrong, but make sure you consider all possibilities. If you are eliminating answer choices and realize that the last one you are left with is also wrong, don't panic. Start over and consider each choice again. There may be something you missed the first time that you will realize on the second pass.

⊘ Avoid Fact Traps

Don't be distracted by an answer choice that is factually true but doesn't answer the question. You are looking for the choice that answers the question. Stay focused on what the question is asking for so you don't accidentally pick an answer that is true but incorrect. Always go back to the question and make sure the answer choice you've selected actually answers the question and is not merely a true statement.

⊘ Extreme Statements

In general, you should avoid answers that put forth extreme actions as standard practice or proclaim controversial ideas as established fact. An answer choice that states the "process should be used in certain situations, if..." is much more likely to be correct than one that states the "process should be discontinued completely." The first is a calm rational statement and doesn't even make a definitive, uncompromising stance, using a hedge word *if* to provide wiggle room, whereas the second choice is far more extreme.

⊘ Benchmark

As you read through the answer choices and you come across one that seems to answer the question well, mentally select that answer choice. This is not your final answer, but it's the one that will help you evaluate the other answer choices. The one that you selected is your benchmark or standard for judging each of the other answer choices. Every other answer choice must be compared to your benchmark. That choice is correct until proven otherwise by another answer choice beating it. If you find a better answer, then that one becomes your new benchmark. Once you've decided that no other choice answers the question as well as your benchmark, you have your final answer.

⊘ PREDICT THE ANSWER

Before you even start looking at the answer choices, it is often best to try to predict the answer. When you come up with the answer on your own, it is easier to avoid distractions and traps because you will know exactly what to look for. The right answer choice is unlikely to be word-for-word what you came up with, but it should be a close match. Even if you are confident that you have the right answer, you should still take the time to read each option before moving on.

General Strategies

⊘ TOUGH QUESTIONS

If you are stumped on a problem or it appears too hard or too difficult, don't waste time. Move on! Remember though, if you can quickly check for obviously incorrect answer choices, your chances of guessing correctly are greatly improved. Before you completely give up, at least try to knock out a couple of possible answers. Eliminate what you can and then guess at the remaining answer choices before moving on.

⊘ CHECK YOUR WORK

Since you will probably not know every term listed and the answer to every question, it is important that you get credit for the ones that you do know. Don't miss any questions through careless mistakes. If at all possible, try to take a second to look back over your answer selection and make sure you've selected the correct answer choice and haven't made a costly careless mistake (such as marking an answer choice that you didn't mean to mark). This quick double check should more than pay for itself in caught mistakes for the time it costs.

⊘ PACE YOURSELF

It's easy to be overwhelmed when you're looking at a page full of questions; your mind is confused and full of random thoughts, and the clock is ticking down faster than you would like. Calm down and maintain the pace that you have set for yourself. Especially as you get down to the last few minutes of the test, don't let the small numbers on the clock make you panic. As long as you are on track by monitoring your pace, you are guaranteed to have time for each question.

⊘ DON'T RUSH

It is very easy to make errors when you are in a hurry. Maintaining a fast pace in answering questions is pointless if it makes you miss questions that you would have gotten right otherwise. Test writers like to include distracting information and wrong answers that seem right. Taking a little extra time to avoid careless mistakes can make all the difference in your test score. Find a pace that allows you to be confident in the answers that you select.

⊘ KEEP MOVING

Panicking will not help you pass the test, so do your best to stay calm and keep moving. Taking deep breaths and going through the answer elimination steps you practiced can help to break through a stress barrier and keep your pace.

Final Notes

The combination of a solid foundation of content knowledge and the confidence that comes from practicing your plan for applying that knowledge is the key to maximizing your performance on test day. As your foundation of content knowledge is built up and strengthened, you'll find that the strategies included in this chapter become more and more effective in helping you quickly sift through the distractions and traps of the test to isolate the correct answer.

Now that you're preparing to move forward into the test content chapters of this book, be sure to keep your goal in mind. As you read, think about how you will be able to apply this information on the test. If you've already seen sample questions for the test and you have an idea of the question format and style, try to come up with questions of your own that you can answer based on what you're reading. This will give you valuable practice applying your knowledge in the same ways you can expect to on test day.

Good luck and good studying!

Development of Motor Skills

Motor Development Processes

Ann Gentile's Motor Learning Stages

Gentile's learning model has two stages. In stage 1, the learner is **getting the idea of the movement.** In stage 2, the learner focuses on **fixation**, or working on consistency and closed skills (e.g., executing the skill in isolation) and **diversification**, or working on open skills in changing environments. In stage 1, the learner is getting a grasp on the movements that are required for the skill. The learner decides on the regulatory and nonregulatory conditions needed to perform the movement. **Regulatory conditions** are important to the movement skill, whereas **nonregulatory conditions** are not. However, nonregulatory conditions, such as crowd noise, can be distracting. Regulatory conditions include things like equipment type, positions of players, and the proximity to the goal. These aspects must be considered before a learner can be proficient. Learners who are more skilled and have more experience are better able to ignore nonregulatory conditions. In contrast, it is difficult for novice learners to ignore nonregulatory conditions. Once learners are proficient, they move on to stage 2.

Fitts and Posner's Motor Learning Stages

Fitts and Posner's three motor stages of learning are the cognitive stage, the associative stage, and the autonomous stage. In the **cognitive**, or beginner, stage, the learner makes lots of errors, is inconsistent, and focuses heavily on the skill cues. During this stage, the teacher is more direct with instructions, which include both verbal instructions and demonstrations, to help the learner understand the movements. This first stage is similar to Gentile's stage 1 (getting the idea of the movement). In the **associative**, or intermediate, stage, the learner has a grasp on the skill and understands the skill movement patterns. This learner will start to become more consistent in movement patterns. As such, they will rely less on skill cues and begin to refine movement by trial, error, and feedback, which aids in the development of self-correction skills. During the associative stage, the teacher designs the practice activities after identifying the errors and providing corrective feedback. In the **autonomous,** or advanced, stage, the movements become automatic and the student can perform skills independently. The learner is able to self-correct during the autonomous stage. During this stage, the teacher should focus on motivation and design activities that refine the movements.

Open and Closed Skills

While no skill is completely open or closed, **open skills** occur in dynamic environments where things are always changing, like during team sports. There are players, a ball (or object), coaches, and spectators, all of which create an unpredictable environment and impact performance. There are also closed skills within team sports, like a free throw in basketball or a penalty kick in soccer, that illustrate the open-closed continuum. **Closed skills** occur in environments that are stable and predictable, like golf. Closed skills are often introduced when teaching novice learners, so that they can focus solely on the skill, or when teaching a closed and controlled activity, like archery. Activities that are open in team sports are often taught in progression from closed (e.g., dribbling in isolation) to open skills (e.g., dribbling during game play) to increase competency.

Bernstein's Degrees of Freedom Problem

Bernstein's motor learning stages focus on the **degrees of freedom problem**. The degrees of freedom problem refers to the variations that can take place in a **complex movement** because of the number of **isolated types of movement** involved in accomplishing a movement skill. For instance, when a pitcher throws a baseball, his feet, legs, torso, arms, and hands are involved in throwing the ball. Therefore, the goal is to reduce the number of problems that can arise from degrees of freedom that may impede success to achieve the desired movement. Two concepts integral to Bernstein's learning stages are the coordination and regulation of movement. Coordination is the ability to move fluidly with complex movement skills. In throwing a ball, a pitcher starts by winding up the upper arm and back and smoothly translating the throw through the whole arm so that all of the arm muscles involved can contribute to the motion. Regulation is the ability to control individual movements in joints, limbs, and muscles. This usually means working a particular muscle in isolation. To work on regulating motions involved in throwing a baseball, one might attempt to throw a baseball by only using the forearm, or work on the associated footwork without throwing a ball.

Bernstein's Motor Learning Stages

Bernstein's motor learning stages revolve around breaking down motor tasks into smaller pieces to develop **regulation** of individual movements, then integrating them to develop **coordination** between those movements. **Stage 1** is freezing the limbs, which involves regulating as many degrees of freedom as necessary to produce the desired movement. For example, the leg and foot action of an overhand throw might be restricted so that the novice learner can focus on the arm motion of the throw. **Stage 2** is releasing the limbs as degrees of freedom gradually increase as skills become more proficient. **Stage 3** is exploiting the environment, (expert stage), which is when the learner is able to perform the tasks in a variety of situations. For example, throwing at different speeds, throwing while running, throwing at various distances and levels, and throwing with defenders all exploit the environment in different ways. Developing skills on each of these levels helps to isolate inefficient movements and develop the fluidity of movements involved in a complex skill.

Motor Learning and Motor Performance

Motor learning is the study of skill acquisition processes and includes the factors that help or hinder motor skill performance. Motor learning can be a permanent or semi-permanent change. Once a person learns how to ride a bike, they will not forget—even after a long absence of riding. Motor learning cannot be observed directly. Instead, performance is observed over time to evaluate consistency and proficiency in a movement skill, which aids in making a determination about whether or not learning has occurred. **Motor performance** is the demonstration of a skill or set of skills. In contrast to motor learning, motor performance is not permanent, as it is contingent upon other factors. While one may have learned how to perform a jump shot in basketball, the success of the jump shot will differ based on the changing environment. Further, the individual's fitness level, fatigue, stress, and other factors impact performance. In contrast to motor learning, motor performance can be observed.

Knowledge of Performance and Knowledge of Results

Knowledge of performance is the quality of a performance. It is often felt by the learner while executing the movement or observed while watching the movement. These feelings or observations help to identify errors that need correction and actions that need to be replicated to promote consistent performance, a process known as **descriptive feedback**. For example, the hand positions and release of a basketball during a free throw can be observed. If the hand position and release of the basketball are to the left, the ball will likely go in that direction. This observation of performance would warrant a change in technique or positioning to improve performance. The feedback given to correct the error in performance is **prescriptive feedback.** In contrast, the **knowledge of results**, or terminal feedback, is the outcome feedback that occurs after a skill has been performed. An example of the knowledge of results is evident during a free throw shot in basketball or a penalty kick in soccer where the outcome is that the ball either goes in or out. When only outcome feedback (knowledge of results) is given, there is little improvement of motor skills. Conversely, knowledge of performance feedback appears more impactful for improving motor skill acquisition and performance.

Skill Transfer

The three types of skill transfer are positive, negative, and zero. **Positive transfer** is when a previously learned skill benefits the performance of another skill. An example of positive transfer may include performing a forehand in racquetball after learning a forehand in tennis. **Negative transfer** is when a previously learned skill impedes the performance of another skill. An example of negative transfer is someone's knowledge of how to properly swing a baseball bat impeding their ability to learn how to properly swing a golf club. **Zero transfer** is when a previously learned skill has no impact on the learning of a future skill. The skills are usually unrelated (though not always). For example, dribbling in basketball has little to no impact on dribbling in soccer. However, positive transfer is often evident during invasion games (team sports that involve two teams with the goal of scoring an object into a goal) such as these because the offensive and defensive concepts and strategies in basketball and soccer are similar.

Theory of Deliberate Practice

"Practice makes perfect" is a common phrase often used in physical education. This concept is included in the five tenets of **deliberate practice** described here.

- Skills must be developed through practice, even among those with natural ability. While it is often assumed that some students have "natural talent," practice is still necessary for improvement and permanency.
- The frequency of practice and the opportunities to respond must be high for students to master a skill.
- Short duration and high quality practice tends to yield better results, so variety in activities is beneficial. This also keeps students on task.
- Goals or objectives must be established to give students focus and to aid in assessment.
- Direct, early feedback is given to both prevent errors and redirect students towards the goal.

Providing Feedback for Motor Skills

Feedback is the information that teachers provide to students to improve motor skills. Types of feedback include general, specific, positive, negative, and constructive. **General** feedback is vague and not focused on the skill performance. It includes statements like "good job" and "nice shot." **Specific** or descriptive feedback is explicit and focuses on the skill action. An example of specific feedback is, "You demonstrated early preparation of your racket by moving it behind you before striking the ball." **Positive** feedback is praise and focuses on what is correct, while **negative** feedback focuses on what is wrong. Both positive and negative feedback can be either general or specific. **Constructive** feedback gives specific details on what the student is doing incorrectly and explicit details on how to improve. An example of constructive feedback is, "You are standing up too straight during your golf swing. You need to keep your knees bent as you make contact with the ball." Students often perceive constructive feedback as negative, therefore, the three-step **sandwich method** of providing feedback is recommended:

1. Specific **positive** feedback is given on what the student is doing well.
2. Specific **constructive** feedback is given on what is wrong and why or how it impedes success.
3. Specific **positive** feedback completes the feedback loop by giving explicit cues on how to correctly perform the skill.

Types of Feedback

When giving student feedback, multiple approaches should be employed, including verbal (e.g., talking), visual (demonstration, images, video), and kinesthetic (student practice). As students move kinesthetically in physical education, it is often recommended to use the **tell-show-do** method to ensure that verbal (tell), visual (show), and kinesthetic (do) types of feedback are reinforced to optimize student learning. This approach is further enhanced by providing video feedback, a type of visual feedback that is shown to have a significant impact on student learning. Similar to other types of feedback, video feedback works best when accompanied by verbal and visual cues, and must be used consistently to have the greatest impact.

Perceptual-Motor Development

Fleishman's Perceptual-Motor Abilities and Physical Proficiency Abilities

Fleishman's taxonomy of motor abilities consists of perceptual-motor abilities and physical proficiency abilities. **Perceptual-motor abilities** are the sensory motor aspects of how the body interprets and responds to the environment. These perceptual-motor abilities include reaction time, rate control, aiming, manual and finger dexterity, control precision, and arm-hand steadiness. In contrast, Fleishman's **physical proficiency abilities** include both skill-related and health-related fitness components or the physiologic aspects of motor ability. The abilities are less dependent on the environment. Health-related examples of physical proficiency abilities include muscular strength, muscular endurance, flexibility, and cardiovascular endurance. Skill-related examples include coordination, power, speed, and balance. Both motor ability categories influence skill development and motor performance. Optimal performance is increased when both are utilized, which can be developed and refined through practice and training. Further, the rates of development and improvement depend on one's abilities, which are determined by biological and physiological influences.

Perceptual-Motor Development

Perceptual-motor skills are needed to perform the fundamental movement skills. While perceptual motor abilities are genetic, they are developed according to stage of development and through practice. Perceptual-motor development is impacted or enhanced by auditory, visual, and kinesthetic discrimination. **Auditory discrimination** is the ability to differentiate between sounds (e.g., loud or soft, the sound of a cow versus the sound a dog). **Visual discrimination** allows students to differentiate between images (people, sizes, shapes, colors, objects). **Kinesthetic discrimination** is the ability to detect small changes in muscle movement, which involves large gross motor movements. The ability to discriminate in all of these areas will foster perceptual-motor development, whereas the inability in one or more of these areas of discrimination will make it more difficult to develop perceptual-motor skills.

Vision and Coordination

Vision is a perceptual ability that aids in balance and coordination, as the information received through the eyes is transmitted to the muscles and the inner ear, which informs or detects movement and a movement response. As such, vision helps with equilibrium, which then helps during physical activities. Performing an activity such as standing or walking with the eyes closed illustrates the impact that vision has on coordination, as the ability to see the environment reduces the difficulty of movement. Vision training helps with other perceptual-motor skills, including eye tracking, movement precision, reaction time, peripheral vision, improved hand-eye coordination, and improved visual discrimination.

Hearing and Perceptual Motor Development

Similar to vision, the ability to hear also impacts perceptual-motor skills, including reaction time, as the sound alerts or prepares the body for the response (e.g., hearing a ball thrown outside the peripheral view). Activities that start with sound (e.g., verbal command, whistle, bell, horn) require auditory senses to transmit information to the brain, which informs movement. Hearing impairments slow down perceptual motor response. Using hearing to improve perceptual-motor skills often combines verbal cues in unison with tactile learning, or learning through touch, especially for fine motor activities (e.g., catching a ball after hearing "hands out in front" or "get ready").

Relationship Between Awareness and Performance

The kinesthetic system (sensory) involves proprioception and joints, muscles, and tendons, as well as receptors of the skin, ears, and eyes. It is largely responsible for body awareness and spatial awareness. Exposure to activities that involve gross motor movements combined with multiple sensory experiences (touch, sound, sight) enhances perceptual-motor performances. Perceptual-motor performances include an awareness of the body's position when stationary (e.g., upright, seated) and during movement (e.g., hands out front when falling forward to prevent injury), which requires balance. This is also developed through a variety of kinesthetic experiences.

Factors Affecting Motor Development and Performance

Constraints and Motor Performance

Constraints are boundaries that limit or promote movement options. **Individual constraints** have two sub-categories: 1) structural constraints, which include physical body structures (e.g., height, weight, gender), and 2) functional constraints, which include psychological (e.g., arousal) and cognitive (e.g., IQ) conditions. **Task constraints** include movement goals, game rules, and equipment used in movement and games. Examples of task constraints include ball size (e.g., women's vs men's basketball size) and game rules (e.g., regulation or modified rules). Adjusting ball size can make the task easier or more difficult. **Environmental constraints** include external factors and also have two sub-categories: 1) **physical environment**, which includes the space (e.g., indoor or outdoor), lights, temperature, and weather, and 2) **sociocultural environment**, which includes social and cultural aspects that impact physical activity engagement and may include gender (e.g., beliefs that girls should not be engaged in physical activity or develop muscular bodies), race, ethnicity, religion, and social class.

Albert Bandura's Social Learning Theory

Social or observational learning theory acknowledges that one's behavior influences others and vice versa. Three elements of social learning theory are **modeling** (watching others), **reinforcement** (rewarding or penalizing), and **social comparison** (the evaluation of skills to the model or a peer). For example, demonstrations, which include learning through observation or the ability to follow a model, are social learning theory methods used in physical education settings. The downside of this theory is that teachers are unable to control all observational learning, since students can learn or observe motor skills outside of class. To ensure effectiveness of observational learning, Bandura suggests a four-step process:

1. **Attention**: students must focus instructional or skill cues
2. **Retention**: students need to remember the demonstrated model (reinforced by skill cues and mental imagery)
3. **Motor reproduction**: students must practice or try to replicate the demonstration
4. **Motivation**: the teacher needs to motivate students to increase their desire to imitate the performance. Reinforcement is often used at this stage.

By including these steps, students are better able to achieve both the psychomotor and cognitive aspects of motor skill acquisition.

Impact of Emotional Development on Motor Performance

The ability to control and recognize emotions (e.g., anger, happiness) impacts motor performance. **Emotional self-regulation** is the control of emotions that starts to develop during infancy and becomes more refined by the age of six. **Emotional knowledge** is the awareness of emotions in other people. **Emotional development** is important because students need to manage emotions in order to focus on instruction. Physical activities that foster positive emotions contribute to positive self-esteem. **Self-esteem** is how one feels about themselves. Positive self-esteem can lead to **competence motivation**, which is the desire to continue to engage in physical activities even when difficult. **Self-efficacy** is the belief in one's ability to perform motor skills. Experiences that foster negative emotions can result in low competence motivation, low self-efficacy, and even disengagement or non-participation in physical activities. As such, increasing student successes in physical education classes fosters the development of both competence motivation and self-efficacy.

Psychological Stimulation and Performance

Arousal is the activation of physiological and psychological responses that vary in intensity from resting to extreme happiness. **Anxiety** is a collection of negative feelings that include fear, worry, and nervousness. A person in a state of anxiety is in a state of arousal, but a person in a state of arousal may or may not be in a state of anxiety. As arousal increases, motor performance tends to increase. According to the Yerkes-Dodson **inverted-U hypothesis**, however, after arousal exceeds the performer's optimal level of arousal, performance tends to regress. Some individuals are able to perform well in high-arousal situations, which is dependent on skill level and experience. Those who are predisposed to **trait anxiety**, or anxiety in non-threatening environments, don't do well in high-arousal environments. **State anxiety,** on the other hand, is a temporary state of anxiety and is only triggered in certain situations (e.g., it is experienced when serving a volleyball in front of others but not when serving alone). Those with high trait anxiety, however, tend to have high state anxiety in high-pressure situations when compared to those with low trait anxiety.

Evaluating Motor Skills

Techniques used to evaluate motor skills include observation and comparison to the model or skill cues. Video analysis software (e.g., Coach's Eye) is also effective, as students' skills are performed and recorded, then replayed simultaneously with the model performance or skill cues, which is used to evaluate strong and weak performance areas. Self-assessments, in which the student checks their performance according to the model or cues, can also be used. Comparing pre-assessment and post-assessment levels of skills is another way to evaluate improvement in motor skills. Tracking student performance over time also provides information on the consistency or stability of a performance and evaluates whether students are able to transfer skills or adapt to other situations.

Detecting Errors in Motor Performance

One technique used to detect errors in motor performance is familiarizing students with the appropriate skill tasks. Using videos tends to work best, as they can be replayed and examined closely. Students should practice skills, observe their performance, and compare it to the desired outcome (self-assessment and reflection). During this strategy, students should be encouraged to identify and solve their own skill problem and follow it with practice. Attentional focus cues accompany the video analysis of the skills so that students can develop an understanding and vocabulary for error detection. This technique helps students pay attention to relevant information and begin to detect and correct errors independently.

Providing Corrective Feedback

Research shows that the best approach to providing effective **error-based** or **corrective feedback** is to surround the error-based feedback with positive feedback, which is widely known as the sandwich method. The focus should be on the desired outcome rather than the error. Therefore, providing skill cues to direct students to the appropriate movement pattern should be given. For example, if a student does not pivot the back foot during the overhand throw, the cue might be "squish the bug" for younger students or "pivot the back foot" for older students; both cues tell the students what to do rather than focus on what they are doing incorrectly.

Delivering Effective Feedback

To provide effective feedback, the developmental stage or level of the student must be considered. After consideration of the student's level, the activity (or sport), and the feedback schedule, frequency, timing, and precision should all be considered. The interests and motivations of students are also important. For example, a beginner is more likely to respond well to error correction feedback to help improve the action or skill, while this type of feedback would be ineffective for an advanced student because they are able to self-detect and correct their own errors. For **unmotivated** or disinterested students, feedback that focuses on the performance of correct actions or skills is more beneficial because this type of feedback fosters engagement in the activity. The amount and precision of feedback varies according to student level, where more feedback is generally given to beginners and tapers off as students progress to higher levels. Feedback should also be vague during the beginner stage and become more precise as students improve.

Elements and Characteristics of Movement

Locomotor Movement

Locomotor movements are fundamental movement skills that allow an individual to move from one place to another. There are eight locomotor movements: walking, skipping, jumping, hopping, leaping, sliding, galloping, and running. Children perform most locomotor movements naturally; they are developed through play and practice. Most children are proficient in the locomotor movements by age eight. Learning these skills helps students learn how and where the body moves and aids in movement efficiency. Locomotor movements are used to teach movement concepts, including **pathways** (e.g., straight, zigzag), **directions** (e.g., forward, backward), and **time** and **speed** (e.g., fast and slow).

Non-Locomotor Movement

Non-locomotor skills are fundamental movements that consist of moving without traveling. Bending, twisting, curling, stretching, reaching, pulling, turning, and swaying are types of non-locomotor movements. **Movement concepts** often taught with non-locomotor movements include personal space, levels (e.g., low, medium, high), directions (e.g., clockwise and counterclockwise), and relationships with the body (e.g., shape formation like round, narrow, twisted, symmetrical, and asymmetrical). In addition to bending and twisting, **skill themes** that complement non-locomotor movements include balancing, jumping and landing, and transferring weight. As students become proficient in non-locomotor skills, they combine them with locomotor and **manipulative skills** to develop mature patterns of movement (e.g., run while jumping; walk while twisting, shuffling, or sliding; and stretching to catch a ball).

Rhythmic Activities

Rhythmic activity is the combination of body movements and music or sounds. Common rhythmic activities in physical education include creative movement, dance, and gymnastics. **Creative movements** use the body (with or without sound) to communicate. Creative movement is the cornerstone for dance and gymnastics. Creative movements or creative rhythms are designed to give students the freedom of expression to move to their own beat without the pressures of formalized dance or gymnastics (e.g., staying on beat to music, performing steps correctly, performing a routine). By design, there are no mistakes when students move creatively, which helps foster **self-efficacy**, or the belief in one's ability to perform motor skills.

General Space and Personal Space

The two types of space in spatial awareness are general space and personal space. **General space** is the space that does not belong to anyone and is used for students to travel during activities. It is the area in gymnasiums and athletic fields where students have plenty of room to move freely without touching someone or something. **Personal space** belongs to the individual—no one should invade another person's personal space. Personal space is private and is often described as an "arms-length" distance. It is recommended that personal space is taught first because this concept can be taught using non-locomotor movements (bending, twisting, marching in place), which gives students time to focus on and develop awareness of how their bodies move without distraction or interference.

Kicking and Dribbling

Kicking and dribbling are **manipulative skills** because the learner manipulates a ball or a piece of equipment. Manipulative skills are more difficult to grasp because they are used alongside locomotor and non-locomotor movements. Kicking is the act of striking an object, such as a ball, with one foot. Kicking is used in games and sports like soccer, kickball, and football. Foot dribbling, which is small, rapid kicking used to advance the ball forward, occurs in soccer and speedball. Hand dribbling, which uses the hands to advance the ball forward, is evident in basketball and team handball. When manipulative skills are developed, students are likely to be more engaged in physical activities and sports that use these skills.

Mature Motor Patterns for Jumping and Landing

Jumping is one of the eight locomotor movements. During the jump, the body becomes airborne after pushing off of a surface with two feet and then returns to the surface with a two-foot landing. The two basic jumps include the vertical jump and the horizontal jump (broad jump). A mature horizontal jumping pattern is when the learner bends the knees, swings the arms back, and then swings the arms forward in unison with the jump. These actions help the jumper propel forward.

Bent knees and the arm swing are the same for the vertical jump, but the jumper's arms swing upward instead of forward. These actions help the jumper propel upward. The **landing** in both jumps require soft or bent knees to absorb the force of the ground and protect the knees. Learning the basic jumps helps with positive transfer of jumps used in sports and other physical activities. Jump patterns and techniques vary among sports and sometimes are actually hops (one-foot take off) like in the long jump, triple jump, and high jump sporting events. Other types of jumps include jumping jacks and tuck jumps. Jumps are also present in jump rope, basketball, volleyball, baseball, diving, and performances on a trampoline.

Overhand Throw

The **overhand throw** is a manipulative skill that involves propelling an object (usually a ball) with one hand above the shoulder. There are generally three phases to the overhand throw: the preparation phase, the execution phase, and the follow-through. In the **preparation phase**, the non-throwing side faces the target and the arm is back with a high elbow. The action of bringing the arm back with the elbow leading is often referred to as the **wind-up phase**. During the **execution phase**, a step is taken with the opposite foot as the elbow leads the arm forward. During this phase, the trunk of the body rotates internally towards the target. The final phase of the overhand throw is when the arm **follows through** diagonally across the body. A one-handed overhand throw is used in several sports, including baseball, softball, basketball, football, and team handball.

Striking Skills

Striking with an implement is a manipulative skill where an object (e.g., ball) is struck with another object (e.g., racket, paddle, baseball bat, golf club). The implement becomes an extension of the user's body. Striking with implements is taught during the latter part of elementary school as hand-eye coordination and visual tracking are needed to produce mature motor patterns. There are two objects that students have to focus on: the implement and the ball. This increases the complexity of the skill. Striking with body parts (e.g., hands) followed by rackets and paddles is the recommended progression to prepare students to strike with an implement. Longer implements (baseball bat, golf club) increase the difficulty of the skill and should be taught last. There are a variety of physical activities that involve striking with an implement, including golf, baseball, tennis, pickleball, badminton, cricket, and racquetball.

Promoting Student Motor Development

Using Animal Walks to Aid in the Development of Movement Skills

Animal walks are fun, simple activities that help students develop gross motor skill movements (locomotor and non-locomotor). Animal walks help students gain understanding of body awareness, body control, spatial awareness, effort, directions, and levels as only the body is needed to accomplish them. Animal walks allow students to use their imaginations by drawing on previous animal movement knowledge and experiences. Teachers can also check for movement concept understanding by seeing how students respond to animal cues. Examples of animal walk cues include "walk like a sloth," to illustrate the concept of slow movement; "move like a cheetah," to illustrate the concept of fast movement; "show me how an elephant moves," which illustrates a large shape and slow speed; and "slide like a snake," which illustrates a low level and curved pathway. Students also develop strength ("crawl like a bear"), cardiovascular fitness ("run like a fox"), and improve flexibility ("stretch like a dog") from engaging in animal walks, which are needed for more complex skills like chasing or fleeing.

Promoting Students' Development of Manipulative Skills

Manipulative activities require the interaction of gross motor and fine motor skills. Strategies used to build manipulative skills include using a variety of manipulable objects. For example, when teaching catching and throwing, different sizes, shapes, and textures of throwing objects should be used with varied distances, targets, and speeds. Performing manipulative skills without locomotor movements before adding locomotor movements also aids in the development of manipulative skills and provides a foundation for game-play actions. An example of this would be to have students start by playing a stationary passing game, then follow that with a game that requires students to run three steps before passing.

Chasing, Fleeing, and Dodging Games

Students should be introduced to chasing, fleeing, and dodging skills after they have demonstrated proficiency in the locomotor movements. Students should also have an understanding of spatial awareness, as chasing, fleeing, and dodging are more complex and require combination movements that often include manipulative skills. It is ideal to teach these activities outdoors to give students plenty of space for safety. Clear boundaries also help facilitate these skills. Tag games are often used to develop chasing, fleeing, and dodging skills; participants flee (running) and dodge (bending or ducking) to avoid getting tagged by one or more chasers. These movements further promote and enhance the movement concepts of **effort** (speed), **relationships** (with others), and **space** (movement with others within boundaries), which are the skills needed to participate in manipulative games (e.g., basketball, soccer, tennis). As such, these are the foundational elements of defensive and offensive strategies.

Using Partner Activities to Teach Locomotor and Non-Locomotor Movements

Strategies used to teach locomotor and non-locomotor movements during partner activities include mirroring, matching, and leading and following. **Mirroring** is when partners are positioned face-to-face and one partner copies the other, **matching** is when partners are positioned side-by-side and one partner copies the other, and **leading and following** is when one partner leads and the other follows. Traveling while mirroring, matching, and leading and following are other strategies used to teach locomotor and non-locomotor movements in pairs. It can be beneficial to have students who are proficient in the movements lead first in order to help the developing students learn the mature movement patterns.

Refinement of Manipulative Skills

Developmentally appropriate techniques that can aid in the **refinement of manipulative skills** include demonstrations, written and verbal cues, feedback (peer, self, teacher), and video analysis. To further aid in the refinement of manipulative skills, multiple objects with various shapes, textures, and sizes should be used, as well as activities that combine fine and gross motor activities. Student choice and gradual progressions (easy to difficult tasks) increase student motivation to participate in skill development activities. There should also be ample opportunities for students to practice or to respond, in order to refine skills. This also requires an adequate amount of equipment, often at a 2:1 ratio. Station practice can be used to facilitate the refinement of skills in isolation at various learning stages, and small-sided games allow students to put skills into practice.

Refinement and Integration of Rhythmic Activities

Teacher-led movements aid in the refinement and integration of rhythmic activities. This technique allows students to follow the movements of the teacher. Students can also create their own movement patterns or routines by incorporating the movement concepts and integrating locomotor, non-locomotor, and manipulative skills. For example, students might be given 6–12 criteria that include the fundamental movement skills and movement concepts. These may include tasks such as four locomotor movements, two rolls, two body shapes, two levels, four balances with different bases of support, and ending on two feet. This example includes both locomotor and non-locomotor movements and several movement concepts, but may also include equipment like balance beams, balls, and ribbons. For students struggling in any of the respective skills, **modifications** or **remediations** should be used. For example, if a student is unable to perform a forward roll, a cheese mat may be useful to give the student more force to turn around the axis of rotation while providing more cushion than regular mats. A student might also use a beanbag between the chin and chest to keep the ball-shaped position needed for the forward roll, which makes it easier to rotate. For students who excel in the forward roll, they should be given additional challenges or **extensions**, like performing a dive roll or multiple rolls in succession.

Locomotor Skill Integration and Refinement

Using **movement concepts** (spatial awareness, effort, relationships) along with locomotor movements will aid in skill integration and refinement. Adding movement concept tasks helps move students from the basic locomotor movements to more mature movement patterns that are used in games, sports, and other physical activities. Examples of movement concept tasks include walk fast, walk slow, walk on your tip toes, walk on the low beam, walk on the high beam, walk in a circle, walk in a zigzag pattern, walk clockwise, and walk counterclockwise; jump high, jump low, jump over, jump alone, and jump with a partner; crawl under and crawl in a circle; hop on top and hop over. Another technique is to combine locomotor and non-locomotor movements. For example, run to the cone, touch your toes, leap and hold, and jump and turn. Participation in **small-sided and tag games** also aid in the refinement of locomotor skills by giving students optimal opportunities to practice skills. Students are also challenged to transfer movements performed in isolation to performing the skills with obstacles, defenders, boundaries, and rules. Game play criteria requires students to integrate locomotor and non-locomotor movements and movement concepts independently, which fosters thinking and decision-making.

Refinement and Integration of Non-Locomotor Skills

Incorporating the movement concepts (spatial awareness, effort, relationships) will aid in the refinement of non-locomotor movements. Movement concepts help students move from the basic non-locomotor movements to more mature movement patterns that are used in dance, gymnastics, and other physical activities. Examples of non-locomotor movements and movement concept tasks include bend one leg, bend two legs, bend one arm, bend your fingers, bend your head up and down (showing the relationship with the body, personal space, and levels); balance on one or multiple body parts, balance on your tip toes, balance in a squat position, twist right, and twist left (showing relationships with the body and objects, direction, and levels). Another technique is to combine non-locomotor movements, which helps with skill integration. For example, balance on one foot while bending the support or non-support leg, or raise and extend (levels and balance) one arm and the opposite leg forward (direction).

Combination Movement Patterns

The overhand throw is a multi-action skill that combines non-locomotor actions with a manipulative skill. Without a ball, all of the movements in the overhand throw are non-locomotor (e.g., non-traveling position, with bending and extending the arm, twisting the torso, and pivoting the foot). The rear or throwing foot pivots simultaneously as the arm, hips, and trunk rotate towards the target. Body weight is evenly distributed on both feet before throwing actions start. The lead foot lifting prior to taking a step forward causes the body to lean slightly sideways, which transfers the thrower's body weight to the rear foot and the body is balanced momentarily on one foot. As the lead foot takes a step and lands, the balance and weight transfer to the lead foot until the follow-through motion is completed.

Balance and Weight Transfer During the Forward Roll

The forward roll combines non-locomotor and traveling skills. Movement concepts involved in the forward roll include shape formation (C-shape), balancing on different bases of support and weight transfer (hands, feet, back), and effort (speed). Students should be competent in basic weight transfer tasks before performing the forward roll. Students can practice weight transfer tasks that include foot to foot, from the feet to the hands, and in rocking motions. These actions can progress to being performed on or with equipment or being held to balance longer. Rolls that are generally taught before the forward roll include sideways (log and pencil rolls) and the forward shoulder roll. Before teaching the forward roll, students should be strong enough in the arms to support their bodies to reduce the risk of neck and back injuries. Cues to help students perform the forward roll include: 1) squat or crouch down in a C-shape, 2) chin to chest, 3) hips up, 4) push-off hands and feet, 5) keep the body tight, 6) roll onto feet.

Agility and Balance

Agility is the ability to move quickly in various directions while maintaining control. Agility is evident in most physical activities and sports. An example of agility is running or shuffling quickly in a zigzag shape, which is a common skill pattern performed in basketball and soccer. Agility is also evident during invasion games when players quickly transition from offense to defense. Agility requires coordination, speed, and balance. **Balance** is what keeps the body stable and upright, which helps keep the body under control. Balance is often highlighted in dance and gymnastics, but agility more broadly is also evident in these activities when performers quickly change directions during sequences.

Common Combination Steps and Sequencing Used in Line Dances

Line dances are dances that can be performed in large groups without a partner, and include locomotor and non-locomotor movements. Basic line dance steps include steps forward, backward, clockwise, counterclockwise, diagonally (three steps and tap), right and left (step touch), or sideways (step-together-step). The grapevine, shuffle, rock steps, taps, half-turns, and quarter-turns are also frequently used. The music used for most line dances is a 4/4 beat, which is a medium to fast tempo. Steps are counted to a 4/4 beat, which usually ends with a tap before changing directions.

An example of a basic step sequence is:

1–4 counts/beats	Walk/step forward and tap
5–8 counts/beats	Walk/step forward and tap
9–12 counts/beats	Grapevine right
13–16 beats	Grapevine left
Repeat	

Verbal Cueing

Verbal cues reinforce desired movement outcomes and help students perform and improve movement skills. **Verbal cues** are action verbs that should be just a few words or less, usually three or four words, as students are better able to focus their attention and remember short phrases.

Example cues for the overhand throw:

Cue	Desired skill outcome
Squash the bug	Reminds students to pivot as they conduct overhand throw
Pick up the telephone	Wind up phase for the overhand throw
Buckle your seatbelt	Follow-through diagonally across the body

Verbal cues are more effective when coupled with demonstrations and written or visual cues.

Kinesthetic Feedback

Kinesthetic feedback utilizes proprioception to relay messages from muscles, tendons, and joints to the spinal cord to respond to movement commands. "Intrinsic feedback" and "knowledge of performance" are other terms used for kinesthetic feedback. Kinesthetic feedback allows the performer to feel the movement, which helps skilled performers correct errors. Performers can only correct feedback for slow movements which occur at subconscious and conscious levels. When movements are slow, smooth, and continuous, like walking on a balance beam, they are subconsciously compared to previous motor patterns, which aids in the refinement of the skill or routine. At the conscious level, the movements are slow, jerky, or both slow and jerky, like when performing a squat. As such, the kinesthetic feedback is conscious and coupled with visual feedback. Therefore, if one squat was ill-performed, the performer has time to correct the errors before performing another squat. Kinesthetic feedback can be improved through practice and refined by also providing visual feedback (pictures, video) and verbal cues to help with the execution.

Video Analysis for Feedback

Video recordings have shown to be more beneficial than other types of feedback because students can watch a demonstration or see their actions and movements, especially when slowed down. Videos can also be replayed. When students are able to view their own performance, it provides instant feedback on the quality or knowledge of performance (technique, skill execution), which other visual aids cannot do. Further, students often believe that they are performing a skill correctly until they view their performance. Video analysis is often considered the gold standard when giving feedback, but to increase effectiveness, it should be used consistently and be paired with verbal feedback. Teachers can also post video demonstrations and analysis online for students for ongoing review to further develop skill competencies.

Movement Concepts and Biomechanical Principles

Movement Concept of Flow

Flow is the contrast between smooth and jerky movements, and the contrast between free and bound movements. **Smooth** movements are fluid, and cues often used to convey this concept are "glide," "melt," and "ooze." In contrast, **jerky** movements are rigid, and cues used to describe this include "rough" and "bouncy." Another type of smooth movement is **free**, in which the movements appear as if the movement is controlling the body rather than the body controlling the movement. An example of free movement is a dancer or an ice skater who spins seemingly effortlessly, or someone running downhill without the ability to stop. These movements tend to be fast, which reduces the amount of control the performer has over their movements. In contrast, **bound** movements are always voluntary and controlled, and they appear tense or stiff at times, like when lifting a heavy object.

Biomechanical Principles Involved in the Leap

Biomechanical principles that are evident during the leap include **power** and **force.** The movement concept categories that are evident are **spatial awareness** (moving through general space), **effort** (force of the leap), and **relationships** with the body and surface. **Power** is strength multiplied by speed (strength × speed), which is generated by the amount of leg force (effort) used during the push-off phase of the leap. The **center of mass** is the equal distribution of the body's weight, which is illustrated during the airborne and landing phases of the leap. Children need to be aware of the relationship of their bodies in-flight and at a medium or high level (spatial awareness).

Movement Concepts of Time and Force

Effort is the movement concept category that includes time, force, and flow. **Time** is either fast or slow, which is the speed, beat, or pace in movement. Fast and slow are often illustrated through dance movements to different music tempos. Distance events like cross country or 100-meter runs and the timing of actions when striking a pitched ball are also evidence of time in physical activity and sports. Changes in time are elicited when the teacher provides opportunities for students to increase (acceleration) and decrease (deceleration) speed at different rates. Force is either strong or light. **Force** is evident in every physical activity because skeletal muscle force is required to move the body. However, the appropriate amount of force to use when performing a certain task (e.g., striking a pitched ball) is learned through practice. Example cues of force are "stomp hard when you walk" or "walk like a feather," illustrating and contrasting strong and light forces.

Spatial Awareness and the Movement Concept of Spatial Directions

Direction is one movement concept under **spatial awareness** (where the body moves). There are several **directions** or routes the body can take that include traveling forwards and backwards, clockwise and counterclockwise, right and left, up and down, and diagonally. **Spatial directions** are often grouped and taught in pairs (e.g., forwards and backwards) for better conceptual understanding. Proficiency in the directions helps build a strong foundation for combining movement patterns that occur during rhythmic activities and team sport transitions (offense to defense), which often require agility or the quick change in direction.

Movement Concept of Relationships with Objects

Similar to directions, **relationships with objects** are often grouped in pairs and include on and off, under and over, behind and through. Relationships with objects are taught before relationships with people because there is more predictability with objects. Objects used in physical education include balls, balloons, scarves, cones, ropes, hula hoop boundaries, goals, discs, and targets. These skills are taught alongside locomotor (e.g., walk behind your ball) and non-locomotor (e.g., stand behind your ball) movements. Activities that involve objects allow for fine and gross motor developments that are needed in more complex manipulative activities and games (soccer, basketball).

Biomechanical Principles in Sports and Physical Activities

Exercise biomechanics and **sport biomechanics** involve the study of forces (internal and external) that impact human movement during physical activity and sports with the goal of improving performance. Biomechanics focuses on improvements in technique, equipment, training, injury prevention, and rehabilitation. Common units of measure used in biomechanics include length (how far or long), time (how much time it takes to complete a task), and mass and inertia (weight and resistance of a body or a piece of equipment).

Buoyancy and Drag in Swimming

Buoyancy is the ability to float in water or air. **Drag** is the amount of resistance that occurs in the air, water, and the body that can negatively impact one's buoyancy. **Body type,** or the amount of muscle mass and fat mass in the body, is critical for buoyancy. For example, fat mass floats more easily than muscle mass, therefore, students with more muscle mass and little fat will have a more difficult time staying afloat and an easier time sinking than students with less muscle mass and more fat mass. To compensate for drag from the water and body, swim techniques are designed to keep the body afloat, including arm strokes, leg kicks, body position, and breathing techniques. Staying in a **streamlined**, or straight, position and synchronizing breathing with strokes also helps one stay afloat. Relaxing muscles and not fully filling the lungs with air also aids in buoyancy and reduces drag.

Physical Laws in Movement

Newton's first law of motion is the **law of inertia**, which states that the objects or the body will continue to move or remain unmoved until met with an unbalanced force. The **moment of inertia** is the difficulty in getting a body or object to rotate around an axis. The goal is to reduce the moment of inertia. During the forward roll, the performer pushes off, or applies **force**, with the hands and feet, which moves the body forward and increases **angular velocity,** or the increase in speed around an axis (or the angle turned through per second). The **moment of inertia** will depend on the position, size, and speed of the performer to determine how easy or difficult it will be to roll. Making the body small and compact, with the chin tucked in, and pushing off with great force makes it easier to roll forward because this increases the **angular momentum**, or the **angular velocity** multiplied by the **moment of inertia**. The rolling motion will continue until met with greater force of the feet or body landing on the floor or mat.

Role of Gravity in Balance and Stability

Gravity is an external force that attracts a body or object towards the earth's center and is commonly referred to as the gravitational pull. **Balance** is the ability to stay in an upright position or maintain equilibrium and an equal distribution of body weight on all sides. **Stability** is the body's ability to regain balance after displacement. Stability is impacted by the size of the base of support, the weight of the object, and the height of the center of gravity. Since the body is dynamic, its center of gravity can change. As such, the body is able to accomplish stability by changing stances and body positions during movement activities. For example, while surfing, the surfer (body weight) has to bend the legs and extend the arms (a change in body position) with a wide stance (a change in stance) on a surfboard to maintain stability and prevent falling.

Force Projection and Absorption

Absorption is the body's ability to absorb or reduce the kinetic energy of an object by applying negative force (e.g., catching a ball). The force is absorbed in the muscles, which helps protect the bones. Another example of absorption is when landing from a jump. The distance or height of the jump can impact the amount of force that can be absorbed; if that force is too great (e.g., jumping from a 10-story building or into an empty swimming pool), injury and potential death can occur. For some activities, the body is unable to safely absorb kinetic energy, therefore, additional absorption is created. For example, safety measures used to prevent injury include sand added to the long and triple jump pit, and the mat used for high jump landing.

Biomechanical Principles in the Overhand Throw

Biomechanical principles used during the wind-up, release, and follow-through phases of the overhand throw include force, torque, acceleration, and the angle of release. **Force** is mass multiplied by acceleration ($F = m \times a$), or the amount of push or pull of an object or body. **Torque** is the force used during twisting actions that often cause rotation. Torque is evident at the shoulder joint during the wind-up phase or external rotation. Torque is also evident during the twisting action or internal rotation of the abdominal trunk during the follow-through phase. **Acceleration** is an increase in speed, and **deceleration** is a decrease in speed. Acceleration occurs during the release of the ball, which is often called the speed of release. The **angle of release** is also evident, which is the point that the ball is released at the shoulder joint.

Biomechanical Errors for an Overthrown Ball

An overthrown ball is often the result of throwing too hard (applying too much force), the angle of release being too large, performing little to no follow-through, or a combination of these errors. To correct the overthrown ball, right-hand students should release the ball at the 2 o'clock position as if facing a clock on the wall, and 10 o'clock for left-hand students to adjust the angle and the timing of the release. "Buckle the seat belt" is a cue that can be used for students to follow through diagonally across the body of the throwing arm. This can also be represented by the 7 o'clock position for right-hand throwers and 5 o'clock for left-hand throwers. The follow-through helps with speed, but also keeps the ball in line with the target.

Biomechanical Errors in a Free Throw

A missed free throw can be the result of the shooter lacking upper body strength or leg strength, so that the force applied is not enough for the ball to reach the rim. There may not be enough flexion in the knees to aid in more power. The shooter may be shooting from the palm of the hands rather than rolling the ball upward and across the hand. The student might also be shooting upward instead of up and outward. If maturation is the problem, the student can try to shoot the ball underhanded between the legs (a.k.a. the "granny shot"), as more power will be generated, thereby giving the ball more lift force. If maturation is not the problem, the student can be cued to "bend the knees," "bend and jump," or "bend and extend" for more power. Releasing the ball at an angle between 50 and 60 degrees may also help the student achieve the goal.

Biomechanical Principles in the Forehand in Tennis

The biomechanical principle most evident in the tennis forehand is torque. **Torque** is the twisting force shown in the external and internal rotation during the racket preparation phase of reaching back (external rotation) to the contact and follow-through phases (internal rotation). **Force** is also evident when the racket makes contact with the ball, which is also under the movement concept **effort**. The striking of the ball sends or projects the ball forward (**projectile motion**). The **timing** of the strike is also a movement concept under the effort category. **Spatial awareness** is evident as the player needs to position themselves to make contact with the ball, and the player illustrates relationships with the self (body awareness); the racket and ball (objects); and, if playing against an opponent, the relationship with another. The player may further illustrate spatial awareness by the direction, pathways, and levels based on the angle of the stroke and desired placement of the ball.

Spatial Concept of Pathways

Pathways is a movement concept under the space and spatial awareness (where the body moves) movement concept category. There are three pathways or patterns the body can create when traveling:

- Straight, meaning to walk in a straight line
- Curved, or moving in a C-shaped or bent pattern or motion
- Zigzag, or moving in a Z-shaped or alternating diagonal pattern or motion

These movement concepts are taught alongside locomotor, non-locomotor, and other movement concepts (e.g., speed, directions, levels). To help students conceptualize and apply pathways, pictures of pathways should accompany the definitions, cues, and phrases used. Associating pathways with previously known information like animals, letters, and gym floor lines also aids in understanding. For example, "walk in a circle" conceptualizes a curved shape, whereas "travel in a 'Z' shape and repeat" would help students understand a zigzag shape.

Spatial Concept of Levels

Levels are a movement concept under the space and spatial awareness (where the body moves) movement concept category. The body can move at three levels: low, or below the knees (crawling on the ground); medium, or between the knees and shoulders (walking); and high, or above the shoulders (walking on tiptoes). This movement concept is taught alongside non-locomotor movements first, then progresses with locomotor and other movement concepts (e.g., pathways and direction). To help students conceptualize and apply the concept of levels, pictures of examples of the three levels should accompany the definition, cues, and phrases used. Associating the levels with previously known information like animals or the other concepts aid in understanding. For example, "stretch your hands high towards the sky" conceptualizes a high level, while "lie down on your back like a mat" illustrates a low level.

Qualitative Biomechanical Analysis

Qualitative biomechanical analyses are commonly used by physical education teachers and coaches. There are generally four steps in a qualitative biomechanical analysis that are used to improve movement skills:

1. Develop a description of the best technique and decide on the desired movement to be observed.
2. Observe the student's performance to determine how the student performs.
3. Compare the student's performance to the desired movement and identify and assess errors.
4. Provide feedback and inform the student with skill cues and other information to correct the errors.

Biomechanical Principles Needed to Maintain Balance

The key biomechanical principles involved in **balance** are the stance, base of support, and the center of gravity. The **base of support** is the area below a person that involves each point of contact or the parts of the body that are in contact with the surface. For example, when standing, the base of support is the area where the feet are in contact. In a push-up position, the base of support is the area where the hands and feet are in contact. A narrow base of support (e.g., standing on tiptoes) raises the center of gravity and reduces the area of support, thus limiting stability or balance. Adjustments (leaning forward or backward) are made during different activities (forces) to prevent falling. A wide base of support with bent knees is the ideal position for balance as the center of gravity is lowered, thus aiding in stability and the prevention of falling.

Improving Body Mechanics for Safe and Efficient Movement

Injury prevention, rehabilitation techniques, and equipment are improvement areas of focus under the study of biomechanics. Sporting injury prevention techniques identified through biomechanics research include bending the knees on landings during gymnastics and adapting the tennis backhand technique to include a neutral wrist position that reduces tennis elbow (overuse). An advance in equipment includes running shoes that provide more cushion to absorb more force. Teachers and coaches also demonstrate an understanding of these principles by taking measures such as requiring the use of mats when students practice tumbling skills and the wearing of shin guards during soccer.

Movement Concepts and Creative Movement

Movement concepts help students take simple movements (locomotor and non-locomotor) and make them more dynamic and interesting to create an aesthetic appeal. The movement concepts give students additional guidance on how and where the body can move. For example, walking in a zigzag pathway allows for more dimension of the movement than walking in a straight line. Forming different shapes (V-shape, X-shape, round shape) while combining locomotor and non-locomotor movements also helps with the aesthetics of movement. Further aiding in the aesthetics of creative movements are the concepts of fast, slow, high, medium, low, jerky, and soft. These concepts help students get comfortable with and refine the fundamental movement skills necessary for dance.

Running Patterns in Team Sports

In team sports, running patterns are "forward and straight" and "forward and zigzag." Running or jogging backwards may occur during transition play (offense to defense and vice versa). At times, a runner's path may be curved into a clockwise or counterclockwise direction when a player maneuvers to receive a pass or to avoid a defender. Running tends to be fast, but may slow down to a jog or walk. There are also a lot of start and stop patterns (e.g., run-stop-run, run-walk-run, run-jog-run), so runs are intermittent. Runs often change directions quickly, which illustrates agility skills used in these sports.

Throwing Patterns in Basketball and Team Handball

While both basketball and team handball are invasion games that use throwing (or passing) to advance a ball down a court or field, the throwing actions used in each game differ. In basketball, most throws are two-handed chest, bounce, or overhead passes. Sometimes players use one hand to bounce or chest pass, but this technique reduces the power of the pass and is often discouraged. Although a one-handed overhand pass can be used to advance the ball far down the length of the court, it is seldom used. In basketball and team handball, a player has the option to shoot, dribble, pass, fake, or pivot after receiving the ball. In team handball, one-hand overhand throws are most common, however, players sometimes use underhand throws. One-hand bounce passes, chest, and baseball passes are also used. Unlike basketball, which uses jump shots and layups to score, the overhand throw is used to score in team handball against a goalie. The scoring differences are due to the position, size, and height of the goals in each respective sport.

Jumping Patterns Used in Sports and Physical Activities

Jumping occurs in volleyball, basketball, and jumping rope. It is also central to the high jump, long jump, and triple jump in track and field. Most jumps are vertical, including jump shots and rebounds in basketball, blocking and spiking in volleyball, and while jumping a rope, which consists of an up-and-down motion. Horizontal jumps, however, occur during the standing broad jump, long jump, and triple jump, where the body is propelled forward during the jump. Although the long and triple jumps have a one-foot take-off and two-foot landing, they are still considered jumps. Similar to the track and field jumps, the layup shot in basketball has a one-foot take off and two-foot landing pattern.

Jumping is both an offensive and defensive skill. It can be used to score points in basketball (jump shot) and volleyball (spike). Jumps are also used to prevent opponents from scoring and to gain or maintain possession of the ball (e.g., blocked shot, rebound). Some jumps have a runup or step approach like a layup or spike, while others do not (e.g., jumping rope).

Kicking Patterns Used in Sports

Kicking is a manipulative skill that involves striking a ball, object, or body with the foot. Kicking is evident in soccer, kickball, and football. The basic kicking pattern consists of using the top of the foot (shoelaces) to strike behind the ball. Making contact in the center of the ball keeps it on the ground, while contact below the ball propels it in the air. Like throwing, there is a follow-through motion in kicking, but the kicking follow-through is upward and forward. The hop-step taken by the support, or non-kicking, leg and leaning forward slightly help with power. The placement of the support foot also determines the direction. For example, if the support toes are pointing left, the ball will go in that direction. Soccer skills also include foot dribbling or rapid kicks back and forth between the feet to advance the ball forward. The insides and outsides of the feet are used to dribble in soccer. Punting is a type of kick done for height and distance and is used in soccer and football. The punt consists of kicking a dropped ball and making contact at a 45-degree angle. A step-hop pattern is also used for punting, although the stride is longer.

Chapter Quiz

Ready to see how well you retained what you just read? Scan the QR code to go directly to the chapter quiz interface for this study guide. If you're using a computer, simply visit the online resources page at **mometrix.com/resources719/mtlephysed** and click the Chapter Quizzes link.

Movement Activities

Individual, Dual, and Team Sports and Activities

Conditioning Programs and Skill Progression Techniques

Conditioning is the process of getting the body prepared for the physical demands of exercise and activity. Conditioning practices are designed to increase health-and skill-related fitness. A general conditioning program consists of a warm-up, health-related movements, skill-related training, and a cooldown with stretching. The intensity of conditioning sessions should gradually progress to reduce the risk of injury or overtraining. This gradual increase is call **progressive overload**, where the intensity of the exercise or activity is above the normal limits. Skill progressions are also used to teach sports, where the easiest form of the skill is introduced and gradually gets more difficult. Skill progressions start at the beginner stage and progressively increase to the advanced stage. A skill progression example for kicking the ball in soccer would be to kick a non-moving ball before kicking a ball in motion or with a partner. In softball, one would strike a ball off of a tee before striking a pitched ball. Each skill builds on the previous skill.

Rules and Safety Practices in Individual and Dual Sports

Individual and dual sports often include handheld equipment (tennis racket, golf club) that can increase the risk of accidental injury if not used carefully. Students need to look around to make sure that people or objects are not in their personal space or striking distance so that they do not hit someone or something. Cones or poly spots are items that can be used to space and mark off waiting and playing areas. Spacing and positioning away from target areas is also crucial during target activities (archery, darts). A proper warm-up should be conducted, and the proper shoes should be worn to reduce injury (ankle strain or sprain). All safety rules must be explained, and consequences for safety violations must be enforced.

Defensive Strategies in Invasion Games

Invasion games are team sports where the objective of the game is to advance an object (ball, puck, Frisbee) down a field or court to score a point into the opponent's goal. Defensive strategies used during invasion games include shuffle steps, drop steps, fast transitions, and reducing open space. Strategies used to reduce open space include staying close to the opponent when they are near the goal. The body should be positioned on the goal side to make it more difficult for the opponent to score. The player should also begin with a large angle for passing and gradually decrease it, executing a technique known as closing the passing lanes. Footwork is also important to help the defender travel faster. Shuffle steps are used because they are quick and crossing the feet over one another slows down lateral movement. Drop steps toward the pass are also used to try to intercept or steal the ball. The defensive player should also leave upon the release of the opponent's pass to increase the likelihood of stealing the ball or forcing a turnover.

Offensive Strategies in Invasion Games

While the specific skill actions differ, offensive movements and strategies are similar in most invasion games. Offensive strategies are used to advance the ball forward and maintain position in order to attack the opponents' goal. These strategies commonly include passing, getting open, or creating space. Passing strategies include ball or body fakes, or body feigns, to slow down the opponent. Passes should also be quick to avoid getting trapped or defended. In order to receive a pass, players should get open or create space. To create space, sharp movements, or cuts, are made that may include L-cuts and V-cuts to keep steady motion to avoid the defense stealing the ball.

Movement in these letter formations helps draw the defense away or in the wrong direction. Body fakes and feigns are also effective because they slow down the opposition by confusing the opponent as to the direction of the player. To aid with maintaining possession, screens or picks should be used, which are when a teammate uses their body to block an opponent. All of these strategies aid in the goal of attacking or scoring a goal.

EQUIPMENT IN NET AND WALL SPORTS

Net sports have a net that divides the court in half, and they include striking an object like a ball (volleyball) or shuttlecock (badminton). Some net sports also use rackets (tennis). Wall sports use a ball that is hit off a wall, and some of them also include rackets (racquetball, squash). Standards (portable poles) are often used to set up volleyball and badminton nets, although some gyms are equipped with built-in standards that lift and lower from the floor. Some schools have outdoor courts, but sports typically played outside can also often be played inside gymnasiums. Nets are sometimes interchanged. For example, if volleyball or tennis nets are unavailable, badminton nets might be used and vice versa. Sometimes play occurs without nets or with net substitutes, such as PVC pipes arranged between two cones to represent the height of the net. If court lines are not available, floor tape and cones can be used to establish boundaries.

EQUIPMENT IN COMBATIVE ACTIVITIES

Combative activities include fencing, wrestling, and martial arts. Cardio-kickboxing is a type of combative activity that derived from martial arts. Rather than kicking, punching, or fighting an individual, air punches and kicks are used to improve and maintain health-related and skill-related fitness. Equipment, including punching gloves, mitts, bags, and shin guards can be used. If equipment is limited, station work can be employed or movements can be done without equipment. For example, while one student uses gloves to punch a punching bag, another student can air punch. Students can switch roles after the allotted time so that everyone has an opportunity to use the equipment. Equipment should be cleaned after each use or session to avoid passing germs. Fencing is an extracurricular activity that involves a sword or weapon (foil, epee, and saber), a face mask, and a head-to-toe outfit to protect the body. Wrestling is also an extracurricular activity that involves a thick, large mat; players usually wear a singlet and male players wear a groin cup.

RULES FOR PARTICIPANTS AND SPECTATORS

Rules are important to maintain order and promote good classroom management, which helps keep participants, classmates, and spectators safe. Game rules outline the objectives of the game, player positions, movements allowed, boundaries, and fouls or consequences for infractions (like game ejection after committing a flagrant foul). Game rules also govern the expected attire, including clothing, jewelry, and the type of shoe. For example, athletic clothes and shoes are expected to be worn during sporting events and at fitness or workout centers. These expectations are also evident in many physical education programs. Class or gym rules also foster a safe and positive learning environment. Students should be taught the rules and routinely reminded of them. Rules should also be posted for students, players, and spectators to read. Coaches also have expectations of following the rules and can suffer consequences as well. For example, when coaches exhibit negative behaviors (e.g., yelling at the officials, throwing things, standing when required to sit, or coaching on the court or field itself), consequences of these violations include team or technical fouls (basketball), yellow and red cards (volleyball and soccer), and ejections from the game (basketball, volleyball, soccer).

DISCIPLINE IN SPORTS

Discipline in sports is the adherence to the game rules and the expectations of the coach or teacher. Discipline also involves actions or practice used to improve skill and fitness. Some players and students have great self-discipline and follow all of the rules and the training involved in sport participation. However, most discipline relies on the teacher or coach to enforce consequences for undisciplined behaviors. Physical punishment (e.g., running laps, push-ups) is a form of discipline sometimes used in sports; however, this type of consequence is discouraged. Other types of consequences include the temporary or permanent removal of the activity or a reduction in playing opportunities.

Etiquette in Sports

Etiquette refers to the unwritten rules of conduct that participants and spectators are expected to adhere to. Etiquette helps to promote safety, fair play, and values. **Sportsmanship** is a term associated with sports etiquette, which includes following the rules, "playing hard but fair," accepting the officials' decisions, shaking the opponents' hands after play, and refraining from outbursts or the taunting of players. Wishing the opponent "good luck" and losing without anger are also examples of sportsmanship, as the enjoyment of the game supersedes the outcome. Sports etiquette also includes remaining silent during a free throw, volleyball or tennis serve, and before the start of a track or swim event.

Teamwork in Sports

Teamwork is the collective effort of a group to reach a common goal. In dual and team sports, teammates work together to score or win a game. The level of teamwork is dependent on the players, the coach, leadership (e.g., captains and managers), the size of the team, and the amount of time a team has been together. For example, teams of two have fewer distractions and attitudes to manage than teams of six, 11, or 25. Teams that have been together a long time tend to have better social cohesion (the degree to which groups get along) than newly formed groups. Further, the more things that players have in common (skill, age), the more likely a team is to work together. Task cohesion also helps establish teamwork, as the desire to win is so important by itself that a team is more likely to cooperate with each other in the pursuit of victory.

Appropriate Participant and Spectator Behavior in Sports

Participants are expected to follow the rules of the sport, accept the coaches and referees' decisions, and engage in fair play. In team sports, spectators are expected to make noise and cheer for their team except during penalty shots or kicks. This cannot be rigidly enforced, as spectators tend to make noise during basketball free throws and at other inappropriate times due to excitement. Spectators are expected to be quiet during golf strokes, tennis and volleyball serves, and at the start of track and swim events. Spectators are also expected to refrain from jeers and profanity.

Differences in Etiquette Between Single, Dual, and Team Sports

Etiquette differences between single, dual, and team sports are noise level, attire, and warm-up procedures. In team sports, crowd participation is encouraged; therefore, there is a high level of noise during game play. In contrast, in individual and dual sports, crowd participation is not encouraged during game play, so the noise level is much lower. The attire also varies. For example, a collared polo shirt is expected to be worn while playing golf, but jerseys are worn in team sports. Jewelry is not worn during team sports, but some may be worn during individual and dual sports. Warm-ups also differ. For example, in team sports, opponents tend to have separate warm-up sessions, but in tennis, the opponents warm up with each other (warm-up strokes and practice serves are done collaboratively).

Elements of Successful Performance in Individual Sports

Self-efficacy is belief in one's ability to perform motor skills. Building a performer's self-efficacy positively impacts performance. According to Albert Bandura, self-efficacy can be enhanced through performance accomplishments, vicarious experiences, persuasion, and physiological state. Goal setting also aids in improving self-efficacy. **Performance accomplishments** include the individual reflecting on previous and current performances to set goals on the desired performance. **Vicarious experience** is learning by observing others complete the desired task (modeling). **Persuasion** is a strategy used to encourage the individual, but the individual must respect and value the person (coach, teacher) who is doing the persuading for it to be effective. Last, the **physiological state** is dependent on the individual's arousal levels and their ability to focus on important tasks. Therefore, for a successful performance, the individual needs to be able to focus on important factors and ignore meaningless information (selective attention) to improve performance outcomes. These elements are also effective in dual and team sports, although there are more variables that affect performance to consider, such as teammates.

Elements of Successful Performance in Dual and Team Sports

Successful performance in dual and team sports is enhanced with team cohesion, established team roles, and goal setting, which fosters cooperation. Team cohesion is when all members of the group or team have the same goal (to win), which has shown to positively impact team performance. Cooperation can be developed by having identified roles (captains, positions) and acknowledgement of the benefits of informal roles. Also aiding in cooperation is sharing individual goals, formulating group goals, and including everyone in the decision-making process. Training should also be fun but challenging, which contributes to an athlete's performance and satisfaction. Collectively, these factors are the elements of successful performance in dual and team sports.

Improving Students' Performance in Individual Sports

Modeling, mental practice, and physical practice are strategies used to improve students' performance in individual sports. **Modeling** is observing the desired performance skills with the goal of replicating the movements. This can be done by observing a teammate, coach, teacher, or by watching a video demonstration. **Mental practice**, also referred to as mental imagery and mental rehearsal, is visualizing or thinking about the performance or skills to be executed. Mental practice is more effective when used in conjunction with **physical practice**, or performance of the skills.

Improving Students' Performance in Team Sports

Practice helps students improve performance in team sports. There are several practice types, including variable practice, massed practice, distributed practice, blocked practice, and serial practice. While all of these types of practices can benefit students' performance in team sports, variable practice has been shown to be most effective. **Variable practice** is performing the same skill in a changing or dynamic environment as it would occur in a game setting. For example, when practicing receiving a pass in soccer, basketball, or flag football, the coach would create different angles and distances for receiving the pass to replicate the constantly shifting environment. As such, students are better able to respond to the dynamic situations that occur during game play, thus improving performance.

Developing Teamwork

Strategies that help improve teamwork include program structure, communication, goal setting, and shared responsibilities. The **structure of the program** (practices and games) is designed by the coach and includes team organization (time, day, and location of practices; rules; positions; playing time). **Input** (communication) from all members in the group on goal setting (individual and team), **shared responsibilities** (everyone sets up and breaks down the equipment), and team building activities are additional strategies that improve teamwork. Team building activities include trust falls, high-ropes courses, tug-of-war, the human knot, and spending time together in non-sporting activities, which are often done before sports practices begin.

Improving Skill Combinations

Part practice is a strategy used to improve skill combinations that are low in organization but high in complexity. **Part practice** is the process of breaking down each segment of the skill before combining the whole movement. For example, the overhand volleyball serve has several parts: the stance, toss, footwork, contact, and follow-through. When using a part practice approach, each part of the serve would be taught in isolation. Each element would build on another before combining all of the elements to perform the serve. Small-sided games also help improve skill combinations, as the combination of isolation skills are put into practice and the opportunities to respond are increased. For example, in a two vs. two game of basketball, players have more opportunities to practice combination skills like dribbling and shooting, dribbling and passing, or shooting and rebounding.

Selecting Sports Activities that Promote Performance

The selection of developmentally appropriate sports activities helps promote performance. The national and statewide physical education standards and physical education curricula are organized by scope and sequence. **Scope and sequence** are a gradual building of concepts and skills that consider the development rather than the age of students. Once skills or concepts are learned, they continue to be promoted, thus refining performance. For example, when striking with an implement, starting with a short-hand implement is introduced before a long-hand implement due to the increase in difficulty. As students learn these skills, the skills are revisited and performed in small-sided or real game play to promote skill refinement, which in turn promotes performance.

Simplification to Promote Performance in Sport Activities

Simplification is a method used to break down skills to promote performance. An example of simplification for the overhand volleyball serve would be to use a larger or lighter ball such as a beach ball, move closer to the net, or slow down the pace of the serve to allow more time to perform the movements. As students become proficient with the simplified versions, modifications would be gradually eliminated. Simplifying game rules also helps promote performance. For example, during a volleyball rally, a simplified rule may be to allow the ball to hit the floor one time before making a play to help students work on footwork and reaction time needed to make contact with the ball. This simplification slows down the pace of the game to promote passing skills without a lot of interruptions.

Adaptations and Modifications to Promote Performance in Sports

Adaptations and **modifications** are things that make tasks easier to promote performance. In net activities like tennis, badminton, and volleyball, adaptations and modifications that can be used include lowering the net. In volleyball, the rules can be modified to allow the ball to bounce once on the floor during play to give students more time and opportunities to respond. In tennis, the ball can similarly be allowed to bounce twice. During target activities (archery, throwing), there can be various target distances to accommodate all student levels and abilities. In team sports, the number of players can increase or decrease. Multiple balls can also be used to give more opportunities to respond, and boundaries can be eliminated in both individual and team sports to promote continuous play.

Tactical Games Approach

The **tactical games approach** is a strategy used to teach team sports. The goal is to develop the cognitive aspects of team sports that includes skills, decision-making, and strategies, thus fostering understanding. There is an intentional focus on developing intrinsic motivation. Rather than the direct teaching of skills in isolation that eventually lead up to game play, the tactical games approach uses a whole-part-whole method in which students play the game first after an objective has been presented ("Today, we will focus on how to get open"). The teacher observes student behaviors to determine areas of growth. However, feedback is given in the form of questions (inquiry-based) to the group to help guide the students in solving problems. For example, the teacher might state, "I noticed that Team A had a difficult time getting open. What are some things we can do to get open more regularly?" With the teacher's guidance, students brainstorm and share techniques, then implement them during the next game play session. Game play is paused for a debrief session to discuss if and how the objective was met. Students then practice solutions to the identified problems and return to play to work on implementing concepts, skills, or strategies in the game that were discussed during the debriefing session.

Specificity in Practice

Practice specificity is the practice of skills and movements as they appear in a game rather than in isolation. Practice specificity is often accomplished through small-sided games. For example, in basketball where a game consists of five vs. five, a small-sided game may consist of two vs. two or three vs. three. Instead of 11 vs. 11 in soccer, there may be three vs. three or five vs. five games. A three vs. three game of keep-away could also be used to teach passing and movement skills used in a real game, as the dynamic movements in the skill training mimic game play. The inclusion of a referee or line judge also provides a game-like situation where calls, fouls, and other infractions are being made.

Performance Activities and Non-traditional Recreational Activities

Jazz and Modern Dance

Jazz and modern dance are social dances that require good posture and body alignment, as this is the foundation used in dance. These dances involve constant changes between neutral movements (static or isometric movements that are held for a period of time such as in a stretch) and dynamic movements (active, controlled movements through a full range of motion).

Basic dance skills used in most dance forms include locomotor and non-locomotor movements:

- Bending (non-locomotor)
- Stretching (non-locomotor)
- Rising (non-locomotor)
- Sliding (locomotor)
- Jumping, or leaping (locomotor)
- Darting (locomotor)
- Turning (non-locomotor)

While the steps in jazz and modern dance are similar, as both consist of free and creative movements, jazz dance has faster tempos and more elaborate movements than modern dance, and may include ballet and hip-hop movements. Modern dance tends to include several dance forms, but the movements are more connected to or guided by the music.

Dance Sequences in Folk Dance and Square Dance

Folk dance is a dance form that is the expression of cultural traditions and customs. Folk dances tell stories about a particular group of people, and are part of rituals and ceremonies like weddings, births, funerals, holidays, and social events. Folk dances also express the trials and tribulations marking certain time periods or eras. Sequences and steps used in folk dance include basic dance steps, but they are performed in accordance to the beat of the music. Folk dances are often performed by several couples (pairs) at one time. Steps include step close, step-cross-step (grapevine), step point, step hop, slide steps, and step swing, and the steps repeat along with the music. While some folk dances may be ethnic dances, **ethnic dances** are associated with or originate from a specific ethnic group's culture (African, Asian, European). **Square dance** has explicit dance moves that are verbally called out (by a caller) along with music. Square dance is performed with four couples, called a set, who are numbered 1, 2, 3, and 4. Couples 1 and 3 are the head couples and face each other, and couples 2 and 4 also face each other. Square dances start by bowing or honoring your partner and corner. Some movements are performed as a group, including grand marches. Other movements involve changing partners, such as swing your corner, or steps, including forward and back, do-si-dos, promenades, and circling left or right.

Conditioning Programs for Dance

Conditioning for dance is similar to other forms of physical activity and sport, and should include exercises that address the health-related fitness components. For building cardiovascular endurance and stamina, aerobic dance is effective because it continuously engages large muscle movements needed for dance. Dance also requires muscular strength, muscular endurance, and flexibility, and so a dance conditioning program should incorporate activities that involve muscle contraction and muscle relaxation. Core strength (abdominals and back) is essential for good posture and body alignment is needed for dance. Depending on the goals and needs of the dancer, cardiovascular activities should be done three to five days a week, strength training two or three days a week, and flexibility training four to six days a week.

Safety Practices When Teaching Dance

Safety considerations in dance include posture and body alignment training; a warm-up (to prepare the body for more vigorous activity); dancing on non-slip floors; having students wear the appropriate footwear; providing water breaks before, during, and after dancing; using damage-free equipment; and a cooldown (to return the body back to normal). Other safety considerations include maintaining adequate spacing so that students do not bump into each other, having the instructor positioned to where all students can be seen, or performing dance in a space that has mirrors for multiple angles of visibility.

Equipment Used in Dance

One of the most common types of equipment used in dance is a sound system or device to play music and speakers or amplifier to project the music. Metronomes can also be used to help keep students on beat. Drums, other percussion tools, and musical instruments can be used to create sounds that accompany dance. A microphone aids in voice projection that can be heard while the music is playing. A wireless microphone allows the teacher to move around during instruction. Dances that involve jumps, leaps, and tumbling may be done on mats. Although not required, dance studios or gyms with mirrors provide a visual of the performer and during teacher-led instruction, allowing for all to be seen. Circus arts such as aerial dances require a high level of expertise, as dancers perform while suspended in the air.

Walking, Jogging, and Hiking

Walking, jogging, and hiking are recreational activities that can be done over a lifespan. These cardiovascular activities are non-competitive (though some form of competition does exist for each) and most people are able to participate with little or no equipment. To improve fitness, these activities should be done several days a week and get progressively more challenging. Increasing the frequency (how often), time (duration), or intensity (effort and speed) of an activity, along with setting goals, can help aid in improving outcomes. For example, a beginner may start with walking for 10 minutes and gradually increase the time by 5–10 minutes every two weeks. To increase the intensity, they might walk faster or hike. One may also start with a 20-minute walk and incorporate intermittent bouts of jogging in between (interval training), which also increases the intensity. Accountability measures also help with improving fitness that involve walking, jogging, and hiking, like the use of pedometers or activity trackers to track or monitor step count, calories burned, distance covered, and elevation (for hiking, walking, or jogging upwards).

ORIENTEERING

Orienteering is an outdoor adventure activity designed to teach students how to use maps and a compass by following routes and finding checkpoints. Each checkpoint has a score, with higher point values for increased difficulty (rough terrain, longer distances). Orienteering involves physical activity (running), and students have to learn how to pace themselves (walk, jog, or run without getting fatigued or "running out of gas"). Maps should be in paper format and a handheld compass is used. Teamwork and decision-making are also involved and can be designed for cooperative and competitive engagement. To help build students' skills with maps and compasses, partners or teams can be given short routes. Students can also create their own maps to use throughout the unit. Because an efficient use of time is critical in orienteering, students must know how to pace themselves. Distance by pace is a common technique used to help students establish a proper pace. Set up practice courses of 100 feet and have students count the number of times one foot (right or left) touches the ground. The number of times the foot touches the ground should be divided by 100, or the course length, to get a pace count. Varying the terrain by distance (e.g., a half-mile to one or two miles) can also help students work efficiently, which is called distance by terrain. In descriptive orienteering, maps are not used. In lieu of maps, bearing (the degrees between map points), distance, and descriptive clues are given to help complete the routes.

SWIMMING SAFETY

Water safety guidelines should be taught before swimming skills. Water safety includes the following:

- Never swim alone.
- Jump in water feetfirst.
- Avoid attempting to save someone from drowning if untrained.
- Do not run on pool decks.
- Wear life jackets on boats.
- Avoid playing breath-holding games.
- Wear proper swim attire.

Introductory swimming skills should be taught first and include pool entry and exit, blowing bubbles, opening eyes under water, floating, treading water, and motions or land demonstrations of the swim stroke. The front crawl or freestyle stroke is generally taught first, using the part method because it is a multi-limb activity that includes arm strokes, kicks with the legs and feet, and breathing.

These skills can be broken down. Examples of skill progression include:

- Floating, both on the front and the back
- Treading water
- Breathing (blowing bubbles from the mouth and nose, alternating breathing)
- Alternating arm action (on land, standing in water, and with flotation device)
- Kicking action (holding onto pool wall and with kickboard)
- Front crawl or freestyle practice – putting the skills together

Periodization in Sports Conditioning

Periodization is a structured training program used by athletes that is broken down into three phases.

1. Phase 1 is the **preparation** or **pre-season stage.** This is a stage, lasting three to six months, where athletes prepare for competition. There are two sub-phases:
    a. The **general preparatory** phase, where the focus is on fitness
    b. The **specific preparatory** phase, where training is specific to the skills and techniques needed for the sport.
2. Phase 2 of periodization is the **competition phase,** where the athlete maintains fitness and works on sports skills and techniques that enhance competitive play.
3. Phase 3 is the **transition** or **post-season stage**, when athletes are tired and take time off to recover from the season for about three or four weeks. To maintain fitness during this stage, athletes continue to work out, however, they engage in cross-training activities that differ from their regular sports training

Bowling

Bowling is a recreational activity that involves rolling a ball down a lane with the goal of knocking down 10 pins. It is also a manipulative activity. While bowling pins can be set up in the gym or outside on the ground to help students learn, bowling is generally played at a bowling alley. The bowling ball has three holes, two in the middle for the middle and ring finger and one to the side for the thumb. The **grip** (ball hold) of the bowling ball can cause stress on the forearms, so forearm exercises can be used to strengthen this area. An underhand motion is used to roll the ball using a delivery (approach and release) of one to five steps. The one-step delivery is taught before the other deliveries in progressive order, as it is easier. Students should aim for the pins using an imaginary line from the delivery to the targeted pins. Markers are on the floors at bowling alleys to help guide bowlers. A skills progression example is: stationary, two-hand ball roll; stationary, one-hand ball roll; one-step delivery; and so on. The distance of the pins can also be progressed by starting the pins closer and gradually increasing the distance until they reach regulation distance (60 feet). Lane width can be adjusted as well, from wider to narrower, until reaching regulation bowling width (42 inches).

Importance of Rules and Safety Practices in Various Recreational Activities

In swimming and other aquatic activities, rules are important because people can drown quickly in bodies of water. Pool rules also help keep patrons and participants safe (e.g., prohibiting running to avoid slipping and falling, avoiding swimming in extremely cold water to prevent hypothermia). For road activities (cycling, in-line skating) wearing a helmet protects the skull from injuries and possibly death if an accident occurs. Individuals engaging in road activities should follow all traffic rules to prevent accidents. Appropriate attire helps protect the body from the elements (e.g., light and loose clothing during the heat, and wick-away layers during the cold). Drinking fluids helps prevent dehydration. For hiking, following hiking trails monitored by park rangers, competence in using a map and compass, and hiking with others are important safety measures that prevent one from getting lost. Sharing the hiking itinerary with someone not hiking is a safety measure that can be used in case one does get lost or injured on the trail. Proper hiking gear (boots, socks, and clothing) prevents slippage and weather-related issues (e.g., sunburn, wind, precipitation). It is also best to stay visible and move to the right so faster hikers can progress. Carrying a cell phone, when possible, is another safety measure to use when hiking.

Discipline in Various Recreational Pursuits

To engage in recreational activities, self-discipline is required, especially when no officials, leaders, teachers, or coaches are monitoring practice, training, or safety. Discipline requires that the individual follow the rules of play and engagement along with consistent fitness and skill training that have shown to lead to successful outcomes in recreational activities. Discipline fosters the motivation to train, practice, study the activity, and observe behaviors that will improve performance or outcomes of consistent performance (e.g., cardiovascular fitness). Focusing on the outcome or creating measurable goals and accountability measures (tracking progress, fitness testing, planning) helps instill discipline.

General Sports Etiquette

General sports etiquette practices include:

- Listen to the coach.
- Know the game rules.
- Put forth effort.
- Respect all participants.
- Discuss disagreements, don't yell.
- Be fair (keep score, admit fouls and infractions, make the right call).
- Do not use profanity.
- Be a gracious winner and loser (e.g., no bragging after a win and no sulking after a loss).
- Shake hands at the end of a game or match.
- Help teammates and opponents if they fall or injure themselves.
- Provide words of encouragement to teammates.
- Thank the coach after games and practices.

Safety Practices and Considerations in Recreational Activities

Safety practices reduce or eliminate injury or traumatic experiences that may occur when walking, jogging, or running outdoors. Safety considerations include wearing proper athletic shoes to support the feet and ankles. Clothes that do not restrict movement should be worn. Running with a buddy or in high-visibility areas is recommended to avoid potential harm. Wearing sunscreen and hats can prevent or limit sun damage and lower skin cancer risks. In extreme heat, the coolest part of the day should be chosen to engage in activities. Drinking fluids (water) before, during, and after activity keeps the body hydrated and reduces the risks of dehydration, which can lead to heat exhaustion and heat stroke. More fluids are needed in hotter temperatures. When cold, layering clothes and wearing wicking materials keeps the body warm and dry, which prevents hypothermia.

Supervising Students in Recreational Pursuits

Issues and procedures to consider when supervising students in recreational pursuits include students changing clothes, locker room or change room duties, hygiene, classroom management of large or multiple classes, equipment, taking attendance, and overall safety. To promote a safe environment, the national physical education recommendations for teacher-student ratio is 1:25 for elementary, 1:30 for middle school, and 1:35 for high school. For class sizes larger than this, a request should be put in for a teacher's aide. Routines (roll call, attendance, warm-up, squad lines, teams, groups) will aid in classroom management, but consistency should be employed. Further, positive reinforcement should be used to encourage favorable behaviors, and consequences should be issued for not adhering to routines. If students change clothes, it is important to adhere to all local and state guidelines to ensure that students are safe and have an appropriate level of privacy. As such, a time limit should be allotted, and if a locker room is used, there should be adult supervision to help students move quickly and prevent theft or bullying. Student hygiene can be problematic because students might not shower after physical activity. Providing adequate time and a private space to shower are ways to address this issue.

Instructional Transitions

Issues with instructional transitions involve time and students finishing early. To help expedite transitions, transitions should be planned and written out ahead of time. Clear, quick, and concise start and stop signals ("Go," or a single whistle blow) help speed up transitions. Students who complete activities early can continue and rotate to the next station and repeat until the cue to stop has been given. This transition strategy keeps students engaged. Timing activities instead of giving a repetition prompt can also help manage transitions. For example, students might engage in the activity for two minutes until they are cued to stop instead of completing 10 jumping jacks or kicks, as students will finish at varying times.

Equipment Management Practices

The lack of equipment, cost, transportation, storage, distribution, cleaning, and repairing are common equipment issues that impact physical education programs. Procedures to help with transporting equipment include setting up or organizing equipment in the space one or two days prior to the lesson. Equipment transition time and distribution procedures can also be built into the lesson. Students can help set up, distribute, and break down equipment by groups, teams, or partners. Students can also be assigned or taught to wipe down equipment after each use. If there is not enough equipment to teach an activity or unit, equipment can be made or modified, or multiple activities can go on simultaneously to give students opportunity to engage in the activities regardless of equipment availability. Requesting funding for equipment from a PTA or PTO can also be considered. Storage facilities should be easy to access and secure, and old or damaged equipment should be discarded and replaced when possible. Keeping an inventory to avoid repeat orders should aid in maximizing equipment budgets. Assessing what students want can also aid in utilizing equipment.

Logistics Regarding Facilities, Space, Staff, and Technology

Physical education facilities and teaching spaces are often shared by other classes. Classes also tend to be large and understaffed with limited technology. Team planning should occur to determine who will teach, what will be taught, and where the class will occur (in a classroom, the gym, or an outside field). Team teaching might also be employed for large classes so that one teacher is leading instruction while the other is monitoring student behavior. To accommodate technology needs, professional development with instruction technology (IT) personnel should be requested to discuss the desired technology uses (videography, LCP projector). When recording students, parental permission needs to be granted. Physical education teaching spaces are often interrupted for school assemblies and other non-PE curriculum activities. To reduce the number of interruptions, a yearly teaching plan with a calendar should be made, compared to the school's calendar, and shared with school leadership to avoid scheduling conflicts.

Selecting, Adapting, and Modifying Activities

SELECTING AND MODIFYING ACTIVITIES BASED ON STUDENT CHARACTERISTICS

Students are diverse and vary in abilities and learning styles. It is important to use a variety of teaching methods to increase effectiveness. Asking students their preferred methods of learning might assist with student engagement and learning. Observations and assessment of abilities should help with the differentiation of instruction. From observation and student data, **modifications** (adaptations) should also be used to accommodate diverse learners by making tasks easier or more challenging. For example, allowing students to walk during activities that require a jog, or increasing the speed for students who find jogging too easy. Another modification example is to allow novice students to strike a ball from a stationary tee instead of a pitched ball, whereas a student on the baseball team might practice striking a ball from a pitching machine. The teacher can also incorporate students' personal goals into activities throughout the unit or academic year.

Review Video: Adapting and Modifying Lessons or Activities
Visit mometrix.com/academy and enter code: 834946

SELECTION OF ACTIVITIES AND GAMES BASED ON INSTRUCTIONAL GOALS

Instructional goals are dependent on national, state, and district standards. Content standards help guide the instructional framework; thus, they set the objectives or instructional goals. There are three objective domains:

- Psychomotor
- Cognitive
- Affective

The **psychomotor** domain is where most PE objectives are derived, as the focus is on the motor development of skills (throwing, kicking). The **cognitive** domain is the knowledge and understanding component that should align to the psychomotor domain (explaining or identifying the cues for throwing or kicking). The **affective** domain focuses on values, feelings, and attitudes (assisting with cleanup or helping a classmate perform a skill).

SELECTING, ADAPTING, AND MODIFYING ACTIVITIES BASED ON A RANGE OF SKILL LEVELS

Differentiation is tailoring education to meet each student's needs. During times when individualized instruction is impossible (large class sizes, little instructional time), teachers can create a variety of learning opportunities and experiences to help meet objectives. For example, a teacher can set up beginner, intermediate, and advanced activities that students can choose from. Students may be in all three groups depending on the skills. To ensure that all students are able to work on each skill, the class can be divided into groups that rotate through the type of activity. The difficulty level for practicing can be self-targeted by the student.

Basketball examples:

Skills	Beginner	Intermediate	Advanced
Dribbling	Stationary dribble	Walk and dribble	Run and dribble
Jump shots	5-foot jump shot	10-foot jump shot	15-foot jump shot
Applied practice	Two vs. two	Three vs. three	Five vs. five

In this situation, students would cycle through three stations. When they go to the jump-shot station, students can pick the distance that they think they need to practice to appropriately meet their current skill level. Coaches standing nearby can help students make a better choice if they pick a target that is too easy or too hard for them. This style of variation allows for both differentiation of skill type and adequate variety for each student's skill level.

Selecting, Adapting, and Modifying Activities and Games Based on Exceptional Needs

There are students already competent in the motor skill objectives planned, while others are still developing or may have a disability. **Extensions** are a type of modification that makes tasks more challenging for students with high ability or who are competent in the tasks. For example, a student on the volleyball team may work on jump serves or target serving rather than the underhand and overhand serves during the service unit. These students can also peer-teach to demonstrate their understanding of the skills and movement concepts. There are also simplified versions (**remediations**) of the skill for students who need more time and direction to grasp the tasks or concepts. There are also students who need additional supports or adaptations that include playing basketball in a wheelchair or using a ramp to assist a wheelchair-bound student in bowling. Modifications or adaptations can be task specific (e.g., use a two-handed, underhand basketball free throw for students who have not developed their upper-body strength), equipment specific (e.g., lower or raise the net in volleyball, or use different size balls), or boundary or space specific (e.g., increase or decrease boundaries).

Principles and Benefits of a Physically Active Lifestyle

Cardiovascular Endurance

Cardiovascular endurance is one of five health-related fitness components. Cardiovascular activities involve engaging in continuous gross motor movements that work the heart and lungs. Cardiovascular activities include walking, jogging, swimming, cycling, hiking, and aerobic dance. It is recommended that youth engage in at least 60 minutes of cardiovascular activities 3–6 days a week. Adults should engage in exercise of at least 30 minutes on 5 days each week, or 150–225 minutes per week. Cardiovascular outcomes are enhanced with muscular fitness and flexibility training because they have a synergistic effect (work together in unison).

Benefits of Living a Physically Active Lifestyle

The benefits of living a physically active lifestyle include lowering the risk of diabetes, heart attack, and heart disease, which are the most common causes of death in the United States. Blood pressure and blood cholesterol are also lowered. Further, bones and muscles are strengthened, which lowers the risks of falling or developing osteoporosis. Physical activity increases metabolism, helps maintain a healthy body weight, and helps improve immunity needed to fight off infections, including some cancers. Physical activity also improves mood, reduces stress, increases energy, improves sleep, and has shown to improve academic outcomes.

Circuit Training

Circuit training is a great way to introduce students to multiple types of exercises. Circuit training is a fitness activity made up of 6–10 stations that are used to improve the health-related fitness components (cardiovascular endurance, muscular strength and endurance, flexibility, body composition) and skill-related fitness components (agility, speed, power). Students participate in each activity for a designated time or number of repetitions before rotating to the next exercise. Circuit training tends to be enjoyable because it is non-competitive, provides variety, and allows students to work at their own pace. Music often accompanies circuit training, which has been shown to positively impact student intensity and engagement.

Learning Opportunities that Promote Participation in Physical Activities

Learning opportunities that promote participation and enjoyment of physical fitness activities include engaging in a variety of activities and developing individualized programs that include personal goal setting, feedback, encouragement, enthusiasm, and role modeling. Variety in activities reduces boredom and allows students to engage in activities they will find enjoyable. Individualized programs with personal goals give students ownership of want they want to work on or improve, which increases the likelihood of participation. Encouragement and providing feedback with a positive attitude foster positive feelings among students, which in turn can elicit student buy-in. Students are also more likely to engage in physical activity if the teacher also engages in physical activity.

Physiological Adaptations in Response to Regular Physical Activity

Physiological adaptations that occur from regularly engaging in cardiovascular physical activity include increased perspiration, stronger and more elastic smooth muscles, decreased heart rate, and an increase in both the size and strength of the heart, which increases blood flow and volume. Oxygen transfer (gas exchange) becomes more efficient due to an increase in alveoli and capillaries in the lungs, which aids in an increase in VO2 max or aerobic capacity. There is also an increase of nutrients and glucose to the muscles performing the work. Exercise recovery also improves as it becomes easier to remove lactic acid. Slow twitch fibers (responsible for slow continuous movements) become more efficient as they are easier to recruit by regularly engaging in cardiovascular physical activity. These adaptations aid in lowering the risks of hypokinetic diseases and obesity-related conditions (e.g., diabetes, heart disease, metabolic syndrome).

Health Benefits of Regularly Physical Activity

Engaging in **regular physical activity** increases life expectancy, improves mood, reduces the risk of some cancers, lowers blood pressure, aids in weight loss, and helps maintain a healthy body composition. Physical activity strengthens bones, which lowers the risk of developing osteoporosis, improves mobility and flexibility, and reduces the risk of falling. Regular physical activity has shown to improve mental alertness, judgement, learning, and relieve some symptoms of depression. Heart rate is also lowered by engaging in regular physical activity, and the risk of heart disease goes down. Blood glucose and insulin are also regulated, and diabetes and other metabolic conditions can be managed by engaging in regular physical activity.

Hypokinetic Diseases and Metabolic Syndrome

Hypokinetic diseases result from inactivity or living a sedentary lifestyle. Hypokinetic diseases include heart disease, obesity, diabetes, and stroke. **Metabolic syndrome** is a collection of diseases or risk factors, including high blood glucose, high blood pressure, excessive fat around the waist, and high cholesterol, which increases the risk of heart attack, stroke, and diabetes. Hypokinetic diseases and metabolic syndrome are often referred to as lifestyle diseases or conditions because most can be prevented by engaging in regular physical activity, eating a healthy diet, and avoiding or limiting certain foods (sodium, fried foods) and substances (smoking tobacco and excessive alcohol intake). Engaging in regular physical activity lowers these risks.

Chapter Quiz

Ready to see how well you retained what you just read? Scan the QR code to go directly to the chapter quiz interface for this study guide. If you're using a computer, simply visit the online resources page at **mometrix.com/resources719/mtlephysed** and click the Chapter Quizzes link.

Physical Fitness and Wellness

Major Body Systems and Physical Activity

Musculoskeletal System and Physical Activity

The musculoskeletal system is a combination of the muscular and skeletal systems that is comprised of muscles, bones, and joints. The skeletal system includes bones, cartilage, ligaments, and joints, and provides the body with protection, support, and movement. There are several types of joint movements, but the most commonly used during physical activity are synovial joints, which are moveable joints. There are three types of muscles (smooth, cardiac, skeletal) that make up the muscular system. However, skeletal muscle (voluntary movement) is responsible for mobility and movement via muscular contraction. Muscles are attached to bones and cause them to move, which changes the angle of the joint (increases, decreases, rotates, extends). These components work in unison for movement to occur, thus they are the components responsible for physical activity. Repetitive and consistent use of the musculoskeletal system has a positive impact on fitness, which translates to better health.

Circulatory and Respiratory Systems and Physical Activity

The circulatory system is responsible for blood transport around the body through blood vessels to the heart and lungs. The respiratory system is primarily contained in the lungs and is responsible for oxygen transport and excreting carbon dioxide from the body during physical activity, which is also known as gas exchange. During exercise, respiration increases to accommodate the oxygen demands of the muscles, and circulation also increases to bring more blood to the working muscles. During respiration, oxygenated air is inhaled through the nose or mouth and travels through the windpipe (trachea) to the bronchial tubes, and then to the lungs. The alveoli in the lungs are where gas exchange occurs (deoxygenated blood for oxygenated blood) and carbon dioxide (waste product) is then exhaled.

Digestive and Excretory Systems and Physical Activity

The digestive and excretory systems work in unison. The digestive system is responsible for converting food into energy and transporting nutrients to the body via blood and other tissues. The excretory system is responsible for removing waste, including blood, from the body. The digestive tract includes the mouth, esophagus, stomach, and the small and large intestines and is responsible for excreting urine and feces. During physical activity, the excretory system rids the body of water through sweat and the lungs of carbon dioxide through exhalations. Physical activity strengthens the digestive track, which makes it easier to remove waste.

Immune, Endocrine, Nervous, and Integumentary System and Physical Activity

Engaging in regular physical activity helps boost **immunity** by increasing white blood cells, which help fight off disease. Getting a cold or the flu also become less likely as the body flushes bacteria from the lungs more efficiently. The **endocrine system** is comprised of the pituitary gland (increases bone and muscle mass), thyroid (regulates heart rate, blood pressure, and body temperature; also increases alertness), adrenal gland (aids in anti-inflammatory response and helps regulate hydration), and the pancreas (helps transport glucose to the working muscles). It also regulates insulin, a process that is improved by physical activity. The **integumentary system** is the function of the skin, which is the point where sweat is released, therefore aiding in thermoregulation. As the body heats up during physical activity, the body releases water (in the form of sweat) to cool off and maintain homeostasis. When the body gets too cold, the skin contracts to retain heat. During physical activity, the **sympathetic nervous system** responds and is responsible for the increase in heart rate. As physical activity diminishes or slows down, the **parasympathetic nervous system** slows down respiration and heart rate.

Components of Health-Related Fitness

Muscular Strength and Muscular Endurance

Muscular strength is the amount of force (push, pull, lift) exerted by the muscles, as shown in lifting weights and performing push-ups. **Muscular endurance** is the ability for the muscles to work continuously or repeatedly without excessive fatigue. Muscular endurance is measured through assessments such as the curl-up test. Although these are two separate health-related fitness components, improvement in one will improve the other. For example, if the fitness goal is to increase size and strength in the quadriceps, training would include lifting heavy loads at low rep counts. Muscular endurance would also improve, but endurance would be gained at a slower rate than size and strength. To train for muscular endurance in quadriceps, the load would be lighter and the rep count higher. Again, the quadriceps will get stronger, but would not likely increase in size due to the low weight and high rep count.

Cardiovascular Endurance

Cardiovascular endurance is the ability to engage in continuous physical activity that increases the heart rate and sweat response. Cardiovascular activities use the heart and lungs, which become more efficient with regular engagement. Engaging in cardiovascular activities lowers the risk of heart disease (coronary artery disease, high cholesterol, heart attack), hypertension, obesity, and metabolic conditions such as type 2 diabetes. Cardiovascular activities also improve mood as endorphins ("happy hormones") are released. Blood also flows more freely, which increases oxygen levels, thus making it easier to breathe. The benefits of cardiovascular activities increase as the frequency and time increases.

Body Composition and Flexibility

Body composition is the measure of muscle, bone, and fat in the body. It is commonly associated with a measure of body fatness (e.g., body mass index, body fat percentage). Maintaining a healthy body composition reduces the risks of obesity and obesity-related conditions. Engaging in muscular and cardiovascular fitness activities along with good nutrition help with the maintenance of a healthy body composition. **Flexibility** is the range of motion at the joint. The lengthening or stretching of muscles helps increase flexibility, which helps increase mobility. Flexibility is often overlooked, but it should be developed just as the cardiovascular and muscular fitness components are. Flexibility contributes to more efficient mechanical movements in these health-related fitness components. In addition to increasing mobility, flexibility helps with posture, body awareness, reduces muscle soreness after engaging in other vigorous activities, and reduces the risk of debilitating back pain. Deep stretching along with deep breathing (e.g., yoga) has also shown to also improve mental health and wellbeing. A lack of flexibility increases the risk of poor health, including pain, stiffness, and difficulty performing daily tasks.

FITT Principle

The **FITT** acronym stands for frequency, intensity, time, and type. It is a simple guide to fitness training principles deemed appropriate for children and sedentary adults. **Frequency** is how often one engages in physical activity or exercise. **Intensity** is the difficulty or challenge of the activities (heart rate, load and weight, reps). **Time** is the duration or how long one engages in physical activity per session (20 minutes, 60 minutes). **Type** is the kind of activities chosen (weight training, cardiovascular activities, yoga). When using the FITT principle, favorable physiological outcomes can occur, as engaging in a variety of physical activity several days a week has shown to promote good health.

Warm-Up and Cooldown in Exercise

Conducting a **warm-up** before engaging in exercise prepares the body for more vigorous activity and may reduce the risk of injury. Warm-ups generally consist of bouts of low-intensity activities and dynamic movements, lasting 5–10 minutes, to increase blood flow to the muscles and heart. The warm-up should reflect or be specific to the activities that will be performed. A cooldown also consists of low-intensity activities and helps return the body back to pre-exercise or normal conditions to restore the body's homeostasis (equilibrium, or bringing heart rate and other systems back to normal). The **cooldown** is the gradual slowing down of the more vigorous exercise session. Stretching may or may not be involved in the cooldown, although stretching during the cooldown, when the muscles are still warm, is best. To increase flexibility, static stretching (holding the stretch for several seconds) is preferred during the cooldown as well.

Overload and Progression in Exercise

Overload is performing more work than is normal or putting stress on the body's systems, either of which can produce physiological adaptations. For example, if one mile of walking is the normal activity done throughout the day, then to increase cardiovascular fitness, one would have to walk more than one mile a day or adapt the routine to include jogging or running, either of which would put more stress on the body than what is normal, thus increasing the intensity. **Progression** (a.k.a. progressive overload) is the gradual increase in overload to reduce the risk of injury and to prevent overtraining or overuse, which can demotivate individuals to continue in an exercise program.

Fitness Goals and Planning

SMART Goal-Setting Method

The **SMART** goal-setting method is designed to help individuals create goals, track progress, and have accountability measures. When setting fitness or exercise goals, they should be specific, measurable, achievable, relevant, and timely. For example, a weight loss goal for someone who is 10 pounds overweight might be to lose five pounds (specific, attainable, and measurable) in 12 weeks (attainable within in the time frame). Based on this goal, the person would design a physical activity program that complements the goal and take an inventory of foods that negate this outcome. A pre-assessment and post-assessment of weight would be taken on a scale (measurable) to determine if the goal was met. They could also measure their weight once a week to track progress over time, especially if the goal is met sooner. If the goal is met before the timeline, a new goal would be created.

Review Video: SMART Goals
Visit mometrix.com/academy and enter code: 100378

Designing Effective Health and Fitness Plans

In order to reap the rewards or experience of the physiological adaptations that occur as a result of engaging in physical activity and exercise, the activities must be performed with **regularity**, or consistency. The activities should also be performed with **specificity**, which is achieved by participating in activities that address the desired outcomes. For example, if the goal is to increase muscular strength, then the activities should involve lifting weights (resistance training) at least two to three times a week. For cardiovascular goals, one should engage in cardiovascular activities for 150 minutes a week. To increase flexibility, one should engage in stretching activities at least twice a week. The principle of **individuality** is also important, as it is recognized that fitness training is personal and a host of factors influence engagement and outcome goals (sport, baseline fitness levels). Factors to consider under the principal of individuality include genetics (gender, muscle fiber type), body type and size, fitness levels, personal preferences, personal goals, and different abilities in reaching fitness goals. Given the understanding that students are individuals with different needs, students should have the opportunity to use the FITT principle and teacher's guidance to develop their own goals and the activities that they want to engage in.

Selecting and Evaluating Physical Activities

Creating SMART goals is the first step that should be taken before selecting activities. Once goals are set, activities should be chosen based on enjoyment and proficiency in the skills needed to perform the activities. For example, playing a game of basketball or soccer can also meet cardiovascular goals instead of traditional cardiovascular activities like running or swimming. Monitoring heart rate (e.g., working in the target heart rate zone) is one way to evaluate the intensity and the effectiveness of training, as the resting heart rate lowers as fitness improves. When initially selecting weight training activities, light weights should be used to ensure proper form and reduce the risk of injury. If the weight is too easy, gradually increase weights until the last few reps in a set are challenging. Lifting at a percentage of a one-repetition max (1RM), the maximum amount of weight that can be lifted one time with excellent form, or a predicted 1RM can be used to select an appropriate weight. Although a 1RM can be used to evaluate strength gains, they are discouraged unless the teacher and students have advanced training and understanding. Reflection journals and workout logs also help evaluate progress.

Self-Assessment of Health and Fitness

Activity Trackers

Activity trackers are devices that record step count, distance traveled, minutes engaged in activity, calories burned, and heart rate. **Pedometers** are activity trackers worn around the waist or wrist that track step count and distance traveled. **Accelerometers** measure acceleration, and most also track step count or distance traveled. **Heart rate monitors** measure heart rate or the intensity of activity through heart rate. Some activity trackers measure all of the above, including body position, and some are waterproof and can be used for aquatic activities. Students may not only be challenged and motivated by activity trackers, but they may even have fun using them. Activity trackers also provide instant and continuous feedback that can help students monitor their engagement and make decisions on the frequency, intensity, and duration of their physical activity, which holds them accountable. Heart rate data is specific to the user, which creates potential for a fair environment where students can work in their own target heart rate zones. Data is also objective, which reduces teacher bias in assessments.

Journals and Fitness Logs

Maintaining **journals** and **fitness logs** are writing activities that help students make connections to concepts and apply them. Journals require students to reflect on skills, performance, fitness, and feelings. Journals can also be used for students to respond to questions regarding the relationships between FITT and behaviors to fitness outcomes. Students can also describe how they felt during the exercise ("The workout was easy, so I need to increase my weight," or "I was exhausted and did not complete the exercises because I had little sleep."), which further aids in their understanding of the interrelated components of health and physical activity. Fitness logs record or document activity over time. Students can log minutes engaged in activity (10 minutes on the treadmill), sets, repetitions, and weight (two sets of 12 reps at eight pounds), and types of activity engaged in (weight training, swimming). Logs also provide students with a visual of progress, which can be adjusted as goals are met.

Self-Assessment

Self-assessments help students track their progress, which helps them develop competence in creating their own fitness programs. Self-assessments may include fitness tests (e.g., number of push-ups completed in a certain time frame to evaluate upper body strength or measure endurance) that students can conduct on their own. Self-assessments may also be performance-based (e.g., the quality of the push-up: hands below shoulders, arms extended, 90-degree angle, body flat). The latter is most important because it helps students gain an understanding of the movements before focusing on fitness outcomes. Self-assessments also remove stress, help fight demotivation, and reduce the unhealthy competition that is often associated with group fitness testing and assessments.

Cardiovascular Endurance and Aerobic Activities

Acute Responses to Aerobic Exercise

Acute responses when performing aerobic exercise include an increase in ventilation, cardiac output, heart rate, and stroke volume. However, after longer durations of continuous aerobic exercise, cardiac output occurs at a constant rate. Blood flow is also redistributed during aerobic exercise because during rest, about 83% of the blood is distributed between the muscles, liver, kidneys, and brain. During aerobic exercise, 84% of the blood is redistributed towards the working muscles. This is able to occur because **vasodilation**, or the widening of the of blood vessels, allows for greater blood flow to the muscles.

Differential Physiological Responses to Aerobic Activity

At rest, aerobically conditioned or trained individuals will have lower blood pressure, lower resting heart rate, greater stroke volume, and slightly lower resting cardiac output than an untrained individual. During sub-maximum exercise, the trained individual will have a lower heart rate, higher stroke volume, and lower cardiac output than the untrained individual. During maximum exercise, the trained and untrained individual will have about the same maximum heart rate. The trained individual, however, will have a higher stroke volume and cardiac output. To train aerobically, one can gradually increase the distance, intensity (moving faster or adding power), and frequency of aerobic activity for improvement. Interval training, in which one would engage in short bouts of high-intensity activity, followed by short bouts of rest or lower intensity activity, is also effective.

Exercises that Promote Aerobic Conditioning

Exercises that promote aerobic conditioning include running, jogging, swimming, walking, biking, aerobic dance, jumping jacks, and jumping rope performed continuously for at least 20–30 minutes. However, high-intensity interval training has also shown effective in promoting aerobic conditioning. **High-intensity interval training (HIIT)** is a combination of high-intensity aerobic and muscular fitness activities performed in short bouts followed by a short rest period. **Tabata** is a type of HIIT training with a work interval of 20 seconds followed by a rest interval of 10 seconds. Repeating these intervals for four minutes has shown to be as effective as a 60-minute aerobic session. A general rule for aerobic interval training is the rest time should be half the work time. Other HIIT work-rest intervals include 30/15, 40/20, and 60/30 seconds.

Metabolism and Aerobic Conditioning

Metabolism is the process of breaking down foods and converting them to energy (carbohydrates, fats, proteins) that is needed to sustain life. Carbohydrates are the primary source of energy, followed by fats, which are the back-up system once carbohydrate stores (glucose and glycogen) are depleted. After the glucose (carbohydrates) and glycogen (stored glucose) stores are used during aerobic activity, fat stores become the fuel source needed to continue aerobic activity because it is long lasting. This process is called **fat oxidation,** which is a metabolic process that helps create the energy. Monounsaturated and polyunsaturated (plant-based fats, liquid at room temperature) fats are easier to break down than saturated fats (mostly animal fats, solid at room temperature) due to the slower metabolic and oxidation processes of saturated fats. This is the reason that limiting saturated fats is recommended, especially among those who want to lose weight or avoid adding additional weight. To burn fat in an effort to lose weight, aerobic activity needs to occur long enough or at high-intensity levels to reach the stored fat in the adipocytes (fat cells).

Cardiovascular Recommendations for Elementary-Aged Children

It is recommended that elementary students between the ages of five and 12 engage in cardiovascular activities 5–7 days a week in sessions of 15 minutes or more several times throughout the day to an accumulated 60 minutes. Activities should vary and students should engage in low (stretching, yoga), moderate (walking), and vigorous (biking, jumping rope, games that involve running or chasing) physical activities. Continuous activity and working towards a specific heart rate goal are discouraged, as the goal at these ages is to encourage and promote physical activity.

Cardiovascular Recommendations for Secondary School-Aged Children

Moderate and vigorous cardiovascular activities are recommended for secondary-aged students (aged 11–18 years) three to seven days a week in bouts of 20–60 minutes. Middle school-aged students are not expected to have target heart-rate goals, but are encouraged to use rate of perceived exertion scales to monitor effort and intensity. This is also the stage where target heart concepts are introduced. High school students are encouraged to work at 60–90% of their target heart rate because the goal is not only to promote physical activity, but to teach students how to plan for exercise as adults. Activities should vary and may include participation in individual, dual, and team sports; speed walking; jogging; dancing; swimming; skating; cycling; and even active chores like mowing grass.

Continuous Training

Continuous training is also known as steady state training because the same activity is performed at long durations or several minutes without rest (e.g., jogging, swimming, walking). Although continuous training is not encouraged for students in elementary school, continuous activities that range from three to five minutes with rest is appropriate for the primary years (grades K-2) or unfit students, 10-minute bouts are appropriate for upper elementary (grades 3–5), and 20-minute and longer sessions are appropriate for middle and high school students. A gradual increase in intensity should occur for all groups, and students should be able to take rest and water breaks when they need to. There should also be a gradual decrease in intensity.

Fartlek Training

Fartlek training, also known as "speed play," is a type of interval training that consists of performing aerobic and locomotor movements over natural or rough terrain at varied intervals. For example, if students are running on a cross-country trail or on grass, the teacher or student may randomly decide when to run hard and when to slow down to a jog and walk. This differs from the traditional interval training that has a set work-rest ratio (20 seconds of work followed by 10 seconds of rest). It is a method used in lieu of continuous training that helps students increase aerobic capacity, maintain a steady pace, increase speed, and develop mental toughness. It is appropriate for older elementary-aged students (grades 3–5) and middle and high school-aged students. All locomotor movements are used during Fartlek sessions in elementary school, and the teacher generally controls the intensity and pace. In secondary school, students are expected to control their intensity and pace based on fitness goals, and the locomotor movements consist of running, jogging, or walking.

Using Heart Rates to Pace Activity

Instead of working at a particular pace, **heart rate training** involves changing intensities based on heart rate. A heart rate monitor is used throughout the activity to ensure that the desired heart rate zone is maintained. For example, if the goal is to work between 70% and 80% of maximum heart rate, the exerciser would slow down their speed when the heart rate exceeds 80% and increase their speed when the heart rate drops below 70%. This is a fair training method to use among students because heart rate is unique to the individual. Drastic or abnormal increases in heart rate can indicate an illness, such as a cold or fever, or a potential for sudden cardiac death. Therefore, heart rate training can also alert the performer of a problem to slow down, stop, or seek medical attention.

Heart Rate Monitoring Methods

Heart rate is used to monitor intensity levels during aerobic activities. Methods used to assess heart rate include manually taking the pulse rate or heart rate and using devices that monitor heart rate. Manual heart rate methods include measuring the pulse at the wrist (radial artery) or the neck (carotid artery), which can be done by placing two fingers (first and middle fingers) at the artery locations and calculating the beats per minute, either by counting for 10 seconds and multiplying the pulse count by six, 15 seconds multiplied by four, 20 seconds multiplied by three, 30 seconds multiplied by two, or for 60 seconds. In every instance, the calculation equates to the number of beats in one minute. Ten seconds is preferred after engaging in physical activity or exercise because it is fast and accurate. A 60-second count is preferred to determine the resting heart rate. Elementary students should monitor heart rate by placing their right hand over the heart. To help elementary students understand the concept of intensity, various activities can be set up with pictures and words to convey low ("move like a turtle"), medium (brisk walking), and high-intensity (running) activities.

Talk Test and Rate of Perceived Exertion

The talk test and rate of perceived exertion scales are easy alternatives to measuring heart rate that are used to establish exercise intensity. If one can talk but not sing during an activity, then the intensity level is appropriate; if one can sing, then the intensity is too low; and if one cannot talk or sing, then the intensity is too high. Rate of perceived exertion (RPE) scales are estimates of how one feels while engaging in aerobic activities. RPEs use a rating scale from 0 (extremely easy) to 10 (extremely hard). There are RPE scales designed for children and adults, and the most common are the OMNI and Borg scales.

Rating	Difficulty	Indicator
0	Rest	No effort
2	Easy	Very minimal effort, walking, able to talk and do other things.
4	Moderate	Not too hard. Activity can be done for extended time, and should still be able to talk while performing activity.
6	Hard	Able to sustain for some time, but pushing the cardiorespiratory limit, meaning they won't be able to talk while performing or sustain for long periods of time.
8	Very hard	Not quite full effort, but nearing that level of intensity. Unable to talk or do anything else while performing. Not sustainable for more than a few minutes at the most.
10	Maximum	Short bursts only. When finished, will be breathing very hard and unable to talk until they catch their breath.

Tracking Duration and Distance of Aerobic Activities

Techniques used to measure the duration of aerobic activities are timetable devices that include watches, activity trackers, stopwatches, cell phone timers, and clocks. Techniques used to measure distance include performing aerobic activities in marked areas (e.g., standard track at 400 meters per lap, swimming pool at 50–100 meters per length) or built-in capabilities (e.g., treadmill, stationary bike, elliptical trainer). For aerobic activities that do not have standard measures or equipment (e.g., aerobic dance, walking or running on a street or unmarked area), a pedometer or accelerometer can be used. The purpose of monitoring the duration and distance is to track progress. For instance, at the start of an exercise program, a brisk 20-minute walk may be difficult, but with consistency and time, the brisk 20-minute walk will likely get easier as the body has adapted to the physical stress. Therefore, one will need to either walk longer or increase the pace (jog) to experience similar physiological responses (e.g., increase in heart rate).

Maximum Heart Rate and Target Heart Rate Zone

Maximum heart rate (MHR) is the maximum number of beats the heart pumps per minute and is dependent on age. The formula for computing MHR is 220 minus the subject's age, so the MHR for a 15-year-old is 205 beats per minute (bpm). The **target heart rate zone (THRZ)** is a percentage of the MHR and has a range of low-intensity and high-intensity that is generally 60–90%. As the model below demonstrates, the THRZ for a 15-year-old is 123 bpm to184.5 bpm (formula below).

	Moderate intensity	High intensity
Base number	220	220
Age	-15 years old	-15 years old
Difference	205	205
Intensity	× 0.60 (60%)	× 0.90 (90%)
THRZ	123 bpm	184.5 bpm

Beginners and unfit individuals should work at 60–70% of their THRZ and gradually increase over time. Fit individuals should work at 80–85% of their THRZ, athletes or those with high levels of fitness should aim for 90%, and some elite athletes can aim for 95%. However, working at this intensity for long periods can be dangerous, so interval training is recommended when working at high intensities.

Karvonen Method for Calculating Target Heart Rate Zone

The Karvonen method (i.e., maximum heart rate reserve) for calculating the target heart rate is one of the preferred methods because it takes fitness as measured by resting heart rate (RHR) into account. It is often used as the method for training. The preferred target heart rate under the Karvonen method is 60–75% because working at higher rates can produce lactic acid via anaerobic systems, thus causing fatigue. Using an individual's resting heart rate ensures that the correct intensity is used for adaptations to occur.

A worked example of the Karvonen formula illustrates the differences between a 15-year-old with a resting heart rate of 72 bpm and a 15-year-old with a resting heart rate of 60 bpm.

Age 15 with 72 BPM RHR		Age 15 with 60 BPM RHR	
60 Percent	**90 Percent**	**60 Percent**	**90 Percent**
$220 - 15 = 205$ $205 - 72 = 133$ $133 \times 0.60 = 79.8$ $79.8 + 72 = 151.8$	$220 - 15 = 205$ $205 - 72 = 133$ $133 \times 0.90 = 119.7$ $119.7 + 72 = 191.7$	$220 - 15 = 205$ $205 - 60 = 145$ $145 \times 0.60 = 87.0$ $87 + 60 = 147$	$220 - 15 = 205$ $205 - 60 = 145$ $145 \times 0.90 = 130.5$ $130.5 + 60 = 190.5$

Using Resting and Exercise Heart Rates to Assess Cardio-Respiratory Fitness

Tracking resting heart rate and exercise heart rates over time can aid in determining cardiovascular fitness progress and physiological adaptations. With consistent cardiorespiratory training, the resting heart rate should slow down. The exercise heart rate should also slow down at similar work rates done previously. The exerciser would use heart rate data to determine if and what changes need to be made. For example, at the start of a fitness program, the resting heart rate is 85 bpm. If there has been no change after six weeks of training, then the individual either needs to increase the exercise time, frequency, intensity, type, or a combination of those variables. The participant may also want to get a physical examination to ensure that there are no underlying conditions (e.g., high blood pressure, illness).

Recovery Heart Rate and Cardiovascular Fitness

Recovery heart rate is the time it takes for the heart to return to normal after engaging in cardiorespiratory activities. As the body becomes more conditioned by adapting to the physiological stresses of engaging aerobic activity, the heart will return to normal faster than someone who is not conditioned. A common recovery heart rate assessment is the three-minute step test, which is also used to predict VO2 max. The **Queen's College step test** is commonly used where a continuous step cadence (up, up, down, down) on a 41 centimeter (16.142 inches) high box or bench at a rate of 88 bpm for females and 96 bpm for males for three minutes. After three minutes has elapsed, a 15-second pulse should be taken and multiplied by four to equate 60 seconds, which corresponds to recovery heart rate and VO2 max estimates. Ranges to aim for are 128–156 bpm for females and 120–144 bpm for males. Students can track their recovery heart rates over time to see if they decrease.

Health Risks When Engaging in Cardiovascular Activities in the Heat

Engaging in cardiovascular activities in the heat increases the risks of dehydration, heat cramps, heat exhaustion, and heat stroke. **Dehydration** (a.k.a. hypohydration) is the when the body does not have enough fluids to maintain the body's processes. **Heat cramps** are painful spasms in the muscles due to fatigue or sodium lost via sweat. **Heat exhaustion** is the result of the increase of a negative balance of water resulting from dehydration, and heat stroke is the result of dehydration and thermoregulation failure (the ability to sweat). These conditions can cause **hyperthermia** (overheated body with thermoregulation failure) and lead to death. To prevent these heat and endurance-related conditions, it is best to hydrate before, during, and after activity, and take more frequent water and rest breaks. Engaging in activity during the coolest part of the day and lowering the intensity and time of activity can also reduce risk. Light-colored clothing is recommended because light colors reflect more wavelengths of light and therefore absorb less heat. Exercising in the shade and wearing a hat with a visor is also recommended.

Risk Reduction and Cardiovascular Training

A risk reduction technique to consider when preparing for cardiovascular endurance training is to have a physical examination from a licensed medical professional to ensure that there are no underlying health conditions that can be exacerbated by physical activity. Another risk reduction technique is to complete the Physical Activity Readiness Questionnaire (PAR-Q), which asks questions used to determine if one is prepared to engage in physical activity. This survey consists of yes and no questions, and if one or more questions are answered "yes," a visit to the doctor for medical clearance is typically recommended. Once activity starts, risk reduction techniques include conducting a warm-up, gradually increasing intensity, wearing a heart rate monitor, and performing a cooldown after activity.

Health Risks When Engaging in Cardiovascular Activities in the Cold

Engaging in cardiovascular activities in the cold increases the risks of skin and body temperature dropping, thus creating heat loss that can lead to hypothermia. Another potential health concern is the increased possibility of inducing an asthma attack for those who suffer from exercise-induced asthma. Conducting cardiovascular activities in cold water exacerbates the effects of the cold and can increase the risk of tachycardia (abnormal resting heart rate) and hyperventilation (higher-than-normal respiration rate), both of which are cold shock responses. A rapid drop in skin temperature (jumping into a cold body of water) increases cold shock responses. When swimming in cold water, vasoconstriction (when the blood vessels narrow) occurs and blood flow to the muscles is reduced, which makes movement stiff and more difficult. **Frostnip** (superficial skin tissues freeze) and **frostbite** (cooling and freezing of cells) are other cold-related concerns. To reduce risk, insulated, breathable clothing that draws sweat away from the body is recommended. When performing activities on dry land, layering clothes and removing layers as the body warms up is recommended. A longer warm-up should also be employed.

Altitude and Cardiovascular Exercise

Most physical activities are performed at sea level, or zero feet of altitude. Altitude training is training at least 7,874 feet above sea level (2,400 meters). There are three main physiological changes that occur when altitude training:

- Red blood cell count increases, allowing increases in the oxygen-transport change, which increases blood flow to the working muscles and helps the body move more efficiently.
- Breathing rate increases, which reduces the amount of carbon dioxide, thus reducing fatigue.
- There is an increase in myoglobin, which is a temporary substance that acts as oxygen when oxygen delivery is compromised (e.g., during long, strenuous activities).

These physiological changes, due to acclimatization from training at a different altitude, have a positive effect on cardiovascular performance when returning to sea level.

Carbohydrate Loading

Carbohydrates consist of sugars and starches that are the body's primary source of energy (fuel). Carbohydrates are broken down into glucose (sugar) to be used for energy. Any overage of carbohydrates (glucose) is stored in the muscles as glycogen, which is easy energy to recruit during cardiovascular endurance activities. Therefore, the purpose of carbohydrate (pasta, potatoes, rice) loading before endurance activities is to provide sustained energy for longer periods of time without accessing fat storage, which takes longer to recruit. Carbohydrate loading has shown effective for longer-duration cardiovascular events, such as 90 minutes of running and other long-duration cardiovascular activities. The negative side to carbohydrate loading is that the athlete or performer may increase body weight because more water is retained to adequately store the extra glycogen. Carbohydrate loading is not recommended for most activities because shorter activities do not last long enough for the body to need to metabolize more carbohydrates, so the extra calories will actually work against a person who is trying to lose weight through shorter activities.

Treadmills and Stationary Bikes

Treadmills promote options for walking, jogging, or running without the need for space. Treadmills are great when it rains or is too hot or cold for outdoor exercise, as they replicate, or are specific to, the motions that are performed outdoors. Treadmills also allow for inclines and declines to train different parts of the muscle used when walking, jogging, or running. The speed and resistance can also be adjusted. Stationary bikes work in a similar fashion but for biking. The downside of using treadmills and stationary bikes is that they are not performed on the same terrain as when performing outside, but they are still effective in improving cardiovascular fitness.

Modifications for Cardiovascular Endurance Activities

Modifications for cardiovascular activities can make the activity easier, more challenging, or less impactful. For example, modifications for jogging include brisk or power walking (lowers the intensity and reduces the impact on the knees), running (increases the intensity), or a combination of all three (interval training). All modalities can increase cardiovascular endurance. However, in order to meet similar cardiovascular outcomes as jogging, one would need to engage in walking longer. Modifications for swimming include using a flotation device to stay buoyant to work on arm strokes and kicks, performing the doggy paddle, and water aerobics. One could also hold onto the wall of the pool and practice kicking and breathing. Endurance and interval sports activities can be used in lieu of traditional exercise activities or programs. They can also be used to cross-train and give the body a break from normal routines.

Muscular Strength and Endurance

Abdominal Strength

Muscles in the abdomen are part of the **core muscles**, which also includes muscles in the back, which work in agonist and antagonist pairings. Often referred to as the abdominals, or abs, these muscles aid in stability and posture. A strong core helps with other exercises. The abdominals should be engaged (contracted, pulling the navel towards the back) during abdominal activities. Exercises to work the abs include curl-ups, plank holds, and variations of these exercises. When performing curl-ups and sit-ups, exhalation should occur in the up position when the muscles contract (the work phase). Inhalation should occur when lowering to the down position when the abs relax. To keep contraction throughout the exercise, the head and shoulder blades should be slightly off the surface on the down phase. Bending the neck should be avoided to prevent neck pain. Holding the arms across the chest is a safer option. Plank holds are an isometric exercise that is measured by time (seconds or minutes). Planks also engage the muscles of the back (erector spinae), the deltoids, and the glutes. Ab exercises are usually done at two to three sets until fatigue or a predetermined rep count. Abs are generally trained three or four days a week, and are usually incorporated into a complete workout program. However, they are also indirectly trained as they act as synergistic stabilizers during other exercises.

Lower Back Strength

The **lower back** is used for most activities, as it provides stability. Exercise recommendations for the lower back include plank holds, Superman exercise, pelvic tilts, bridges (glute raises), reverse curls, deadlifts, leaning back, leg lifts, low rows, stretching (cat and cow, lying on back alternating knees to the chest), and windshield wiper with knees. However, it is important to note that lower back injuries are common, so care should be taken to protect it. When lifting items off the floor, the knees should be used to lift and the hips and glutes should be kept back, rather than bending over and lifting with the back. Lower back exercises should be done in a slow and controlled motion. Inhalation occurs during the contraction portion and exhalation occurs during the relaxation portion. For isometric exercises like a plank, inhalation and exhalation are maintained throughout the hold. Lower back exercises should be trained three to four days a week, although lower back stretches can still be performed daily.

Upper Body and Trunk Strength

The **upper body** includes the arms, chest, back, and shoulders. The chest, back, shoulders, and abdominals comprise the **trunk** (body parts above the waist and below the neck). Muscles in these areas should be trained two to three times a week, with at least one rest day between sessions. Types of exercises, the associated muscles, and common exercises are indicated below.

Major Group	Muscle	Recommended Exercises
Arms	Biceps	Dumbbell curls, barbell curls, hammer curls, cable curls, preacher curls
	Triceps	Seated dips, dips, tricep kickbacks (extensions), overhead extensions
Chest	Pectorals (major and minor)	Push-ups, bench press, cable crossovers
Back	Latissimus dorsi and rhomboids	Lat pull downs, seated row, bent row, one-arm row
	Erector spinae	Reverse curls, Superman exercise, deadlifts
	Trapezius muscles	Shrugs, shoulder blade squeezes
Shoulders	Deltoids	Front/lateral/rear deltoid raises, shoulder press – dumbbells, barbells.

Many of the exercises for these muscle groups are also performed on exercise equipment, which tends to be a safe option because machines have more support than free weight exercises.

Leg Strength and Endurance

To train muscles in the legs for strength, high weight and low reps (3–10) should be employed. For endurance, low weight and high reps (10–20) should be employed. Sets generally range from 1-5, depending on the goal: 1–3 sets are often conducted for endurance, and 3–5 sets are often done for strength. Shorter rest times between sets are taken for endurance, and longer rest times between sets for strength. Alternating workouts between strength and endurance allows for focus on each health-related fitness component.

Common exercises that work the muscles in the legs include:

- **Quadriceps**: Squats, lunges, leg extensions
- **Hamstrings**: Deadlifts, hamstring curls
- **Soleus/gastrocnemius**: Heel/toe/calf raises (double or single-leg), seated calf raises

Flexibility and Posture

Promoting Good Posture and Flexibility in the Hips, Ankles, and Knees

Hip flexors are the muscles that, with proper flexibility, make it possible to bring the knees upwards and towards the body (chest). The hip flexors also help with good posture because they aid in spinal stabilization. Sitting for long periods can reduce flexibility, while engaging in certain physical activities (dance, soccer, cycling) can improve it. To increase flexibility in the hip flexors or alleviate "tight hips," hip flexor stretches should be conducted using the hip hinge motion (leading with the glutes moving backwards while the chest leads the forward bending motion) to prevent lower back injury.

Mobility in the ankles work in unison with the hip flexors to maintain posture. As the body stands from a seated position (chair) or bends, the hips hinge while the ankles dorsiflex (toes toward the body). Exercises that help build strength and flexibility in the ankles include alternating between dorsiflexion and plantar flexion (toes pointing downward), ankle rotations, hopping side-to-side on one foot, and balancing on one foot while the other one swings forward and back, then switching sides.

The knees also aid in good posture. To maintain good posture when standing, the knees should be soft (slightly bent), the feet should be placed shoulder-distance apart, the arms should be relaxed and hanging, and the body should stand straight and tall with the shoulders back. During exercises, the knees should also be soft, and locking the knee joint should be avoided. When performing squats and lunges, the knees should be aligned or behind the toes. To protect the knees, avoid hanging them over the toes.

Promoting Good Posture and Flexibility in the Lower Back and Trunk

Lower back stretches that promote good posture and flexibility include child's pose, cobra, upward facing dog, supine twist, and lying on the back and bringing the knees to the chest. Trunk exercises that aid in good posture and flexibility include back extensions, spinal twists, crunches, crunches with a twist, and wood chops. Trunk stretches for flexibility include upper trunk rotations, trunk flexion rotation, standing and seated lateral trunk stretch, seated trunk rotation stretch, and dolphin stretch. For the chest and upper back parts of the trunk, reaching back (stretching the arms) aids in posture by keeping the chest lifted, shoulders back, and back upright. This is a counter-balance stretch because the shoulders and posture can be compromised (shoulders rounded forward, curve in the upper back) when the muscles on the anterior side are stronger than the posterior muscles.

Promoting Good Posture and Flexibility for the Shoulders and Neck

Shoulder exercises that promote good posture and flexibility include reaching the arms back, reverse plank, threading the needle, dolphin, eagle arms, sphinx, and alternating shoulder stretch (hands touching behind the back in opposition). The following exercises are used to increase strength and flexibility in the neck, which also aids in good posture. Neck exercises include tilting the head forward (chin towards the chest), bending or tilting the head towards the left and right (side to side), and rotating the head to the right and left. These stretches should be held for 5–10 seconds and repeated up to five times each. Bending or tilting the head back is not recommended.

Resistance Training to Promote Flexibility

While static stretching is effective for increasing flexibility, it is not the only option for doing so. Weight and resistance training also increase range of motion, thus increasing flexibility. In fact, recent research suggests that strength training is just as effective at increasing range of motion as stretching is. During weight training, especially exercises that include a full range of motion (e.g., push-ups, squats, pull-ups, deadlifts), stretching occurs while building strength. Foam rollers (compressed tubes) are also effective in improving flexibility since they can apply pressure that is able to penetrate deep inside the muscle tissue, which aids in muscle lengthening.

Evaluating Strength, Endurance, and Flexibility

Evaluating Muscular Strength

The steps used to conduct a one-repetition max (1RM) test are listed below.

Pectoral strength measured by the bench press:

1. Warm-up the area evaluated using a light-weight bench press for two to five sets.
2. Use two or three spotters.
3. Select a heavy weight within the limits of the student.
4. The student will bench press the amount of weight as many times as possible. If they can bench press one time in good form without assistance, then that is the 1RM. If they can bench press the selected weight more than one time, they should stop, add more weight, and repeat three to five minutes later. This would continue until the 1RM is achieved.

A safer method to use is the estimated 1RM. Two methods of estimated 1RM are below.

- Use an estimated 1RM table to determine what the 1RM would likely be. For example, students select a weight that they can lift for six repetitions but cannot lift for more than 10 repetitions (chart dependent). If a student performed eight reps at eight pounds, they would use the estimated 1RM table corresponding chart and would find that their estimated 1RM would be 10 pounds.
- Another method is to use the 1RM estimated max formula: (weight lifted × 0.03 × repetitions) + weight lifted = estimated 1RM max. Using the example of a student performing eight reps at eight pounds: $(8 \text{ reps} \times 0.03 \times 8 \text{ pounds}) + 8 \text{ lbs} = 9.92$ pounds, which rounds up to 10 pounds.

Evaluating Endurance

There are two types of **endurance**: muscular endurance and cardiovascular endurance. At times, they work together, like when jogging or swimming; although these activities require muscular and cardiovascular movements, they are classified as aerobic because they use large amounts of oxygen. The amount of time engaged in the activity is how both are measured. For example, timing how long one can engage in continuous movement and tracking trends helps to determine improvement. When participating in locomotor endurance activities, tracking distance is another method used to evaluate endurance. For example, if someone jogs for 30 minutes a day, they can track the distance covered in the amount of time. If the distance increases, the data would suggest they are getting faster and the heart, lungs, and muscles are working more efficiently. Common cardiovascular endurance assessments include the 1-mile run, multi-stage progressive runs, 12-minute runs, and three-minute step tests. Common muscular endurance (and strength) tests are the curl-up test, push-up test, and plank hold. The number of reps completed over a certain amount of time (e.g., two minutes) is another method of evaluation. Muscular endurance activities performed in isolation are classified as anaerobic because little to no oxygen is required to engage in the activity.

Evaluating Flexibility

Flexibility is often evaluated by length or a decrease in joint angle. For example, the sit-and-reach is a test commonly used in physical education programs to measure lower back and hamstring flexibility. The test is usually performed on a box to protect the back, but can also be performed on the floor. In a seated position with the legs extended forward, the goal is to reach towards the feet as far as possible with slight tension but without pain. A tape measure on the floor or ruler on the box measures the distance or the length of the stretch. The back saver sit-and-reach is conducted with one leg at a time (while the other is bent upward). A tape measure is not required, as reaching an area on the body also provides information on progress. For example, one may initially only be able to reach their shins, but with practice they can eventually reach their toes or go beyond their toes, indicating improvement.

Safe and Appropriate Activity for Improving Fitness

Activities for Improving Muscular Strength

Muscular strength can improve with and without equipment. Body weight exercises are generally introduced first because they are safer than exercises that use equipment. Body weight exercises also allow students to become familiar with what the body can do (e.g., body awareness). Some body weight exercises that help build strength are push-ups, curl-ups, planks, squats, lunges, and several variations of these exercises. Exercise tubes, resistance bands, and stability balls also improve strength because they add a little more resistance than body weight training alone. For faster strength gains, kettlebells, medicine balls, and dumbbells can be used. These types of equipment allow the body to complete exercises that mimic regular movements. Weight lifting machines (e.g., hamstring curl, leg press, lat pulldown) allow for heavy weight to be lifted, but restricts some natural movements, which makes it a safe option. Over time with consistency, exercises should get easier as the body adapts, and either the load (weight) will need to increase or more repetitions will be required to see further progress. It usually takes between four to six weeks for adaptations to occur. If the intensity remains the same, the body may plateau, which means there will be no more improvement gains.

Activities for Improving Endurance and Indicators of Improvement

The cardiorespiratory system needs to be challenged at least three days a week for 20–60 minutes for endurance to improve, increase, or maintain cardiovascular fitness. With consistency, the body adapts to the exercises and becomes more efficient and capable of meeting the cardiovascular demands on the body. Activities that help improve endurance include jumping rope, walking, jogging, running, swimming, aerobic dance, HIIT training, road and stationary biking, elliptical trainers, rowing, and high-repetition muscular fitness activities. Indicators of improvement include lower resting and working heart rates, faster recovery heart rate, longer durations, and a decrease in fatigue response. The activities will also get easier to do over time. Using a variety of these activities (a.k.a. cross-training) will prevent a plateau effect by putting different challenges across all body systems (e.g., musculoskeletal, circulatory, respiratory).

Activities to Improve Flexibility and Posture

A warm-up lasting five to 10 minutes is recommended prior to engaging in flexibility and posture activities. Selecting activities depends on the goal. Range of motion (ROM) exercises can be done every day to increase flexibility. ROM exercises are static holds (e.g., touching the toes, grabbing one foot, spinal twist) where the position or posture is maintained for 20–60 seconds. **Proprioceptive neuromuscular facilitation (PNF)** stretching, which is comprised of static holds with a person or object applying pressure to help deepen the stretch, has been shown to be most effective for increasing flexibility. These stretches should be used in intervals of stretch-relax-stretch. Static and PNF stretches are good for physical therapy (rehab for an injury) and are often done at the end of a workout. Static stretching is also preferred for students in elementary school as they learn body awareness. Dynamic stretches are introduced in middle school. Dynamic stretching is often used in warm-ups because it increases blood flow while stretching in positions and movements similar to the workout or sport. In this way, dynamic stretches prepare the body for the specific work.

Progressive-Partner-Resistance Exercises

Partner exercises allow for greater isolation of the muscle than when performing exercises alone. These exercises are also good for students who are too small to use exercise machines. Ideally, partners should be the same height, weight, and ability level (e.g., strength, flexibility). Communication is essential to prevent injury, therefore, the student performing the exercises needs to inform or cue the partner with how much pressure should be applied. The partner that is assisting should provide feedback on technique and form to ensure safe, correct movements. Equipment that can aid in partner-resistance exercises include exercise tubes, bands, and towels.

Principles, Safety Practices, and Equipment for Weight Training

When engaging in weight training, weight selection should take into account the concept of progressive overload (start with a light weight and gradually increase) to prevent injury. A warm-up should also be conducted to prevent the risks of injury. Warm-ups usually consist of performing the same activities with little to no weight and is commonly referred to as a "warm-up set." For example, when conducting the biceps curl, a warm-up set might consist of 20 reps at five pounds before performing the biceps curl at the desired weight of 20 pounds at 10 reps for three sets. General principles include training the same muscle group at least two days a week; high weights with low reps for strength and size; low weights with high reps for endurance; rest between sets (30 seconds to three minutes), taking longer rests for size and shorter rests for endurance; and including at least one rest day between weight training workouts for the targeted body part or muscle group. Below are two **splits**, or weight training workout schedules. Depending on the segmentation and muscle groups to exercise, splits can come in hundreds of different variations.

Sunday	Monday	Tuesday	Wednesday	Thursday	Friday	Saturday
Legs	Arms, shoulders	Chest, back	Legs	Rest	Arms, shoulders	Chest, back

Sunday	Monday	Tuesday	Wednesday	Thursday	Friday	Saturday
Legs, arms	Chest, back	Shoulders, core	Rest	Legs, arms	Chest, back	Shoulders, core

PRINCIPLES, SAFETY PRACTICES, AND EQUIPMENT FOR CIRCUIT TRAINING

Circuit training is a combination of cardiovascular and non-cardiovascular activities performed at stations for a certain number of minutes or repetitions. Circuit training exercises may only include body weight exercises, free weights, resistance equipment (bands, suspension trainers), or a combination. In addition to the normal exercise safety (e.g., warm-up, cooldown, hydration), there are additional safety concerns that must be considered for young children (elementary school-aged). During physical activity and exercise, teachers should be aware that the bodies of young children are less able to thermoregulate due to a lower sweat response than adults, therefore children may overheat faster than adults. As such, young children should be given more frequent rest and water breaks (before, during, and after activity). Their breathing capacity is also lower than older children and adults, which can cause them to hyperventilate, so the intensity should be moderate, not high.

DETERMINE APPROPRIATE INTENSITY OF TRAINING

Appropriate measures used to determine cardiovascular endurance training include training in one's target heart rate zone. The target heart rate zone is a percentage (60–90%) of an individual's maximum heart rate. Once the target heart rate has been computed, it can be monitored by taking the pulse or by wearing a heart rate monitoring device. The goal is to stay within the 60–90% the maximum; beginners should stay in 60–70% and gradually advance to 85–90% in future sessions. The talk test is another way to determine intensity: if the subject is able to talk, but not able to sing during the activity, then they are working at an appropriate intensity. If they are unable to talk, then the intensity is too high, and if they are able to sing, then the intensity is too low. For muscular fitness activities, gauging how one feels during the activities is a method used to determine the intensity of exercises. Whether training for strength or endurance, the last few reps in each set should be challenging but doable. When the last few reps are easy, it is an indication that the weight or rep count needs to increase, thus increasing the intensity.

APPROPRIATE DURATION OF TRAINING

The duration of training is dependent on the goal. For example, if the goal is to complete a 5-kilometer (3.1 miles) race, a gradual increase in distance should occur until the 5-kilometer goal is met. Running or swimming slightly over 5 kilometers can help train the body so that the stress response during the 5-kilometer run is easier. On the other hand, if someone is training for a marathon (42.185 kilometers, or 26.22 miles), multiple longer runs leading up to the marathon are recommended. Given the distance of a marathon, however, it is not recommended to train at or beyond the marathon distance. A few 20-mile runs are a general recommendation when training for a marathon. These recommendations are based on the principle of specificity. If one is training at shorter distances (e.g., 100-meter run), the duration should be short and explosive with repeated trials or attempts. It would be inappropriate to train in short bouts for activities that take a long time to complete and vice versa.

APPROPRIATE FREQUENCY OF TRAINING

The frequency of training depends on goals, fitness level, and the time available to train. For beginners, a training program consisting of two to three days a week at low-intensity activity is recommended. For intermediates, frequency recommendations are three to four days a week of moderate activities. For advanced exercisers, four to seven days a week of vigorous activities. A gradual increase over time has shown the most effective in exercise adherence. For weight training, it is generally recommended to perform two or three sets of each exercise (e.g., push-ups in three sets of 10) two to three days a week. More sets are recommended for those who are focused on size, and the frequency of workouts could be once a week because it will take longer for the body to recover and repair after heavy loads.

Safety and Effectiveness of Training That Promote Strength

Safe and effective training that promotes strength in children and adolescents includes body weight training and lifting weights. It is a myth that children should not engage in strength training, as it was once thought doing so would stunt their growth. Research shows that elementary-aged children benefit from strength training activities, however, the activities should vary to reduce the risk of injury and prevent overtraining. Since children and youth's bones (epiphyseal plate, or growth plate) are still developing, a slow progression should occur. Non-strength activities should be included (e.g., those that improve cardiovascular performance and flexibility). Specialization in training should not occur until later adolescence (e.g., high school-aged). Although multi-joint activities have shown safe for young children, proper form and technique that include slow and controlled movements are a must, as these types of exercises can put additional stress on the shoulder joint and lower back. To ensure safety, and in addition to progressive overload, the teacher should be trained, students should be taught about the benefits and risks, a warm-up should be conducted, frequent water breaks should be given, and rest days or non-strength activities should follow strength-training days. **Contraindications** and risky movements to avoid include jerky movements, locking of the joints, hyperextension, and fast and uncontrolled movements.

Safety and Effectiveness in Endurance Training

Most endurance activities (walking, jogging, running) conducted during physical education are appropriate for K-12 students, however, because of developmental stage, modifications should be made. For example, elementary-aged children should engage in bouts of endurance activities not to exceed 15 minutes at a time, while middle and high school students can engage in longer durations (20 minutes or longer). HIIT training can be used across grade levels, but it is only recommended for students who are moderately fit and should be avoided by students who are not. Swimming activities are effective, although specialized training among personnel is required and a certified lifeguard should be on duty during instruction. Students need to be proficient in floating and swimming or need flotation devices that keep non-swimmers buoyant. Endurance machines are also effective, but are unsafe for elementary-aged students due to size and developmental stage.

Safety and Effectiveness in Stretching

Static stretching and yoga poses are effective in promoting flexibility and enhancing posture. A warm-up should be conducted prior to stretching to reduce the risk of injury. To be effective, stretching should occur at least two days a week and be held for 10–60 seconds to the point of tension (not pain), followed by relaxation and repeat. There should be a gradual increase (progressive overload) in the amount of time the stretch is held. Regular breathing should occur, and during exhalation is the time to try to go deeper or reach farther (in small increments) in the stretch. No more than four stretches per muscle group at three sets each are recommended. Static stretching is recommended for elementary-aged children because it is more controlled and they are still learning how to move the body. Furthermore, dynamic stretching (with movement) can increase injury in young children because they can easily overstretch. Caution should also be used among older populations because static stretching can restrict blood flow and increase blood pressure, as the majority of blood is pooled to the area being stretched. Athletes and students in secondary school tend to warm-up using dynamic stretches, which are mobility exercises that mimic sporting movements and prepare the body for more intense motion specific to the activity.

Diet and Nutrition

Macronutrients

Macronutrients include carbohydrates, proteins, and fats. Macronutrients are energy-yielding nutrients because they provide the body with energy to fuel exercise and physical activity. Water is not an energy-yielding macronutrient, but it does it help transport the energy-yielding nutrients throughout the body. Water is the most essential nutrient because the body cannot survive without it. Carbohydrates (sugars and starches) are the primary source of energy, followed by fats and proteins. Fiber is a substrate of carbohydrates and comes from plant-based foods (vegetables, fruits, and grains). Fiber is either soluble (digestible) or insoluble (indigestible). Carbohydrates are either simple and easy to break down (table sugar, fruits) or complex (pasta and bread). Complex carbohydrates are more filling and supply longer energy than simple sugars. Fats supply long lasting energy after energy from carbohydrates (glucose, glycogen) has been used. Fats are either saturated (semi-solid at room temperature) or unsaturated (liquid at room temperature). Unsaturated fats are better for health. Protein's main role is muscle building and repair. Proteins are found in animal products like meats and eggs. There are also plant-based proteins, including beans, legumes, and soybeans (tofu). Proteins are made up of 20 amino acids, 11 of which are non-essential, as the body can produce them. The remaining nine are essential and can only be obtained through food.

Micronutrients

Vitamins and minerals are micronutrients (small amounts) and are responsible for growth, development, and maintaining the body's processes. Vitamins have two categories: fat soluble (vitamins A, D, E, and K) and water soluble (vitamins B, C, and all others). Having an overabundance of fat-soluble vitamins can be toxic. However, vitamin D deficiency is a concern in the United States, especially among people of color. Vitamin D helps with calcium absorption and is responsible for bone, skin, and immune health, and serves as a protective factor against cancer and other health conditions. Sources of vitamin D include dairy, salmon, and other fatty fish. Sources of vitamin A include carrots, sweet potatoes, spinach and liver. Vitamin E sources include almonds, sunflower seeds, and peanuts. Sources of vitamin K include broccoli, brussels sprouts, and spinach. Minerals also have two categories:

- Macro (calcium, potassium, sodium)
- Micro, or trace minerals (copper, fluoride, iron)

Ingesting too many minerals can lead to life-threatening conditions (e.g., too much sodium can lead to hypertension), so one should follow the recommended daily allowances based on age, gender, pregnancy status, and illnesses or predisposed conditions. Minerals are found in meats, fruits, vegetables, nuts, dairy, and fortified foods (cereals).

Basic Principles of Weight Management

The energy balance equation shown below is a simplified formula to describe weight management. Energy in is the amount of **calories** (unit of energy or unit of measure for fuel) consumed from foods and substances, and energy out is the amount of calories burned from movement or physical activity.

Energy in = Energy out = No change in weight
Energy in > Energy out = Weight gain
Energy in < Energy out = Weight loss

Physical activity patterns impact the equation. For example, individuals who engage in more physical activity will need more calories as fuel. In contrast, sedentary individuals will need fewer calories because inactivity consumes calories at a much slower rate. For individuals who want to gain weight, the energy in needs to exceed the energy out. Those who want to lose weight need to burn more calories than they consume.

Diet and Exercise Patterns

Generally, it is recommended that 45–65% of our diet comes from carbohydrates, which is the primary source of energy. Complex carbohydrates (vegetables and grains such as sweet potatoes and brown rice) are preferred over simple carbohydrates (fruits, desserts, sugar, and fructose) because they take longer to break down, thereby providing longer bouts of energy. 20–35% of a person's diet should come from fats. Unsaturated fats (oils that are liquid at room temperature, including plant-based oils like olive oil and canola oil) are preferred over saturated fats (solid or semi-solid at room temperature such as animal fats, lard, and butter) because too much saturated fat increases the risks of heart disease and obesity. Saturated fat should account for less than 10% of total fat intake. 12–20% should come from proteins, which are made up of 20 amino acids (building blocks of proteins), 11 of which are non-essential (the body can produce) and the remaining nine of which are essential (obtained from the diet foods consumed). The ranges take into account the needs and patterns of the exerciser and include the type of the activity. For example, someone who wants to increase muscle mass should take in more protein, while someone who wants to train for endurance may increase or consume more carbohydrates. In addition to physical activity, calorie intake and the way the body burns fuel is also dependent on genetics, gender, age, and body size and structure. There are online calculators that can provide an estimate of what is needed based on these factors.

Basic Nutrition Principles

The basic nutrition principles include getting food from multiple food groups for a balanced diet. The five food groups include:

- Dairy or dairy alternatives (e.g., milk, cheese, yogurt, soy)—should be low or reduced fat
- Proteins—fish, poultry, lean meats, eggs, tofu, nuts, beans, legumes, seeds
- Vegetables, including beans and legumes
- Fruit
- Grains—rice, bread, cereal, pasta, noodles

Intake of foods from the food groups ensures that the body is getting essential nutrients for the body's processes (systems). Low consumption of fat and moderate consumption of sodium and sugars are recommended because consuming too much of these can lead to obesity, obesity-related illness, high blood pressure, high cholesterol, and type 2 diabetes.

Body Mass Index

Body mass index (BMI) is the most widely used measure of body composition. It is the relationship between weight and height squared. The BMI formula is: weight (kg)/height (m^2), and is used to determine or predict the body fat of an individual.

BMI Categories
Underweight < 18.5 Normal weight $= 18.5 - 24.9$ Overweight $= 25.0 - 29.9$ Obese ≥ 30.0

BMI is the most commonly used body composition measure because it is easy to calculate and non-invasive. However, there are several limitations. BMI is an indirect measure of body fatness because it does not measure the amount of fat in the body. There are also race, ethnicity, gender, and structural differences (mesomorph, ectomorph, and endomorph) to consider. **Ectomorphs** tend to be extremely thin and have a difficult time gaining weight. However, these individuals can also be "skinny fat" and have more fat on the body than appearances suggest. **Endomorphs** tend to be short and stout and have large bones, which can elevate or positively skew BMI. While these individuals carry larger amounts of fat, they are able to build muscle. **Mesomorphs** have athletic builds, tend to be lean, and have large muscle mass, but may register as obese even when they actually have low levels of body fat.

Skinfolds and Waist Circumference for Measuring Body Fat Percentage

Skinfolds are a common measure of body fat percentage which involves pinching certain areas (e.g., biceps, triceps, subscapular, suprailiac, chest, abdomen, thigh) on the body using a skinfold caliper. This method is accurate and inexpensive, but involves touching the skin. The three-site and seven-site skinfolds are commonly used and vary by gender and age. The sum score (measured in millimeters) of the sites corresponds to a body fat percentage. Waist circumference is another measure of body composition and health risks as abdominal fat poses greater threats to good health. Although there are race, ethnicity, age, gender, and body structure differences in appropriate body fat percentages and waist circumference, general guidelines suggest to keep these low and small on respective criteria.

Waist circumference is another measure of body composition, which is also easy and accurate to measure and involves taking a spring-loaded tape measure above the iliac crest to measure the circumference of the waist. Too much fat around the abdominal area increases the risk of metabolic conditions. It is recommended that women maintain a waist circumference less than 35 inches and men should aim for less than 39 inches to minimize health risks.

Diet and Exercise Plans for Weight Management

A combination of physical activity, low-fat, and high-fiber diets aid in maintaining a healthy body composition. Physical activities should include cardiovascular, muscular-strength, and muscular-endurance exercises conducted most days of the week. Cardiovascular activities help burn fat during the activity, and muscular-fitness activities help burn calories during and up to one to three days after. Diets that include consuming vegetables tend to have a positive effect on body composition because these foods are low in calories but are nutrient dense (vitamins, minerals, fiber). Eating lean proteins also aids in maintaining a healthy body composition. Limiting sweets, high-fat foods, and alcohol will help maintain a healthy body composition because these contain large amounts of sugar, fat, and empty calories.

Caloric Approach to Weight Management

Counting calories is a strategy used to help maintain a healthy body composition. To do this, one needs to calculate their basal metabolic rate to determine their caloric needs. The **basal metabolic rate (BMR)** is the number of calories needed to keep functioning at rest. To compute BMR, height, weight, gender, and age are needed. A revised version of Harrison Benedict's BMR formula is below.

Male: $(88.4 + 13.4 \times \text{weight in kilograms}) + (4.8 \times \text{height in centimeters}) - (5.68 \times \text{age})$

Female: $(447.6 + 9.25 \times \text{weight in kilograms}) + (3.10 \times \text{height in centimeters}) - (4.33 \times \text{age})$

Once BMR is established, calories consumed would be counted not to exceed the BMR if the desired body composition is met. For weight loss, either fewer calories or more physical activity is recommended for desired body composition. For weight gain, more calories (ideally from lean proteins) or heavy muscular fitness activities are recommended.

Effects of Various Factors on Health and Fitness

Rest and Nutrition

Resting the body is essential for peak physical performance and good health. Rest includes taking a break (a day off) from training and getting adequate amounts of sleep. Rest allows the body to recover and rebuild from the physical stress of exercise and activity. When the body and muscles are well-rested, performance tends to be more efficient, whereas little to no rest can impede progress. Nutrition is also important for physical performance and good health because poor nutrition (high fat, high sodium, no fiber) negatively impacts growth, energy, exercise recovery, and a healthy body weight. Good nutrition (vegetables, grains, lean protein, low fat) provides energy and allows for greater demands on the body.

Alcohol and Tobacco

Consuming alcohol and tobacco can negatively impact physical performance and health. Alcohol contains empty calories (7 calories per 1 gram of alcohol) and no nutritional value, which can cause unwanted weight gain. Alcohol is metabolized before carbohydrates and fat, which disrupts weight-loss goals. Alcohol is a depressant drug that slows down the central nervous system, so movement responses (e.g., reaction time) are slower. Alcohol also lowers inhibitions and impairs judgment, and when working out, an injury may occur. Excessive alcohol consumption can lead to cirrhosis of the liver (scarring) and alcoholism (addiction).

Nicotine is the addictive substance that is found in tobacco products. Smoking tobacco increases the risk of cardiovascular disease (hypertension, stroke) and makes it more difficult to breathe, especially during physical activity, since blood flow is restricted due to the narrowing of blood vessels. Chewing tobacco increases the risks of tooth loss and throat and mouth cancers. When people stop smoking and drinking, many of the ill effects diminish over time.

Heredity

Heredity (genetic characteristics) impacts physical performance and is the foundation of one's health. For example, abilities (power, reaction time, muscle fibers) are hereditary, and some have more ability than others. While all can improve, improvement will only go as far as one's genetic abilities. The same is true for health, as some people are predisposed or have a higher risk of poor health if conditions and illness run in their family. For example, if a parent has hypertension or diabetes, the offspring are at greater risks. Physical activity and nutrition can help mitigate negative heredity aspects.

Personal Health Risk Factor Assessments

Health risk assessments (HRA) are commonly used to evaluate personal health risk. HRAs contain a battery of questions to help determine areas of health risk. HRA questionnaires tend to ask the age, gender, race, ethnicity, history of depression, physical activity, emotional health, social activities, pain, seatbelt usage, tiredness, injuries, smoking, alcohol consumption, and other questions that pertain to health. Based on the results of the questionnaire, physicians may administer a corresponding health assessment. Today, however, there are also online versions of HRAs that can help one evaluate their own health and make changes according to the results. Another option is to get an annual physical with blood work to receive an annual report on cholesterol, lipid, blood glucose, red and white blood cell profiles, and a host of other factors that can be determined by blood tests. Results provide information on how to maintain or improve health and reduce health-risk factors.

Healthy Choices and Behaviors

Self-Determination in Making Healthy Choices

As children transition from childhood to adulthood, they need to be capable of making healthy choices for themselves. In early childhood, nutrition, sleep, hygiene, and fitness are almost solely in the hands of parents. As children age and make more decisions for themselves, they can vary the amount and types of food they eat, the time they sleep, and what types of activities they participate in. Usually by middle school or high school, students have enough decision-making power over their own lives that they are really controlling their own fitness and health. It is essential to provide students with the knowledge of what types of choices there are to make and how their choices affect them in the short term and in the long term. For instance, students may not consider how sleep habits affect them, but may decide to make better choices if they realize that sleep deprivation has powerful effects on one's mood, weight management, and stress level. Self-monitoring strategies, such as a health journal or calorie-tracking applications, may be helpful in encouraging students to increase their own self-awareness and pick good goals for themselves.

Patterns in Health Choices

Habits are when a behavior choice becomes repeated enough that those choices become the default way of acting. As good habits are formed, the choice involved becomes less difficult to make, as it becomes the natural pattern. Many healthy choices are difficult to make because they require effort or sacrificing something, such as time or instant gratification. Most health choices involve short-term sacrifices to achieve a long-term result, such as losing weight from skipping snacks or candy bars every day. The ultimate result is usually very rewarding, but requires considerable effort in the short-term. Key elements to successful habit-forming are to make sure that the goal is visible and that the behavior is consistently repeated. For example, if a student wants to lose weight by skipping sugary snacks, it is best not to cheat on the diet by occasionally having a candy bar. Cheating on the diet would undercut the development of a desired good habit. The goal also must be visible. If a student cannot see progress from their efforts, then they will not feel rewarded by their hard work and will struggle to maintain it. In this situation, it should be encouraged that the student keeps records of their initial weight or size and track the changes over time to see how well their behavior choices are affecting their outcomes.

MAINTAINING A HEALTHY WEIGHT

Choices that aid in maintaining a healthy weight include engaging in regular physical activity rather than sitting, taking stand-up breaks or moving every hour instead of sitting for very long periods throughout the day, choosing a low-fat diet over a high-fat diet, and eating baked foods instead of fried foods. Taking the stairs instead of the elevator or parking the car far away from a destination rather than close can increase physical activity, which burns calories and helps with weight management. Choosing to have at least three vegetables a day instead of none will increase fiber and nutrients, which also aid in weight regulation. Choosing to eat sweets in moderation (once a week instead of seven days a week) and adhering to serving size recommendations (rather than all-you-can-eat consumption), or eating smaller portions, further support healthy weight maintenance.

Effects of Stress and Stress Management

STRESS AND ITS EFFECTS ON THE BODY

Stress is the body's response to the demands placed on it. Stress can be either physical or psychological (mental, emotional), and it can be either positive (eustress) or negative (distress). The stress response is usually fight (confront and deal with the stress) or flight (run away or avoid the stress). Chronic stress can have damaging mental and physical effects on the body, including high blood pressure, obesity, diabetes, heart disease, heart attack, stroke, anxiety, body aches, insomnia, irritability, fatigue, chest pain, sadness, depression, and a sense of being overwhelmed.

TECHNIQUES FOR MANAGING STRESS

Techniques or strategies that help manage stress include getting adequate sleep (8–10 hours per day), meditation, daily physical activity, deep breathing, yoga, tai chi, laughter, and mindfulness (awareness of behaviors and responses). Progressive relaxation (alternating between tensing and contracting muscles or releasing and relaxing muscles), guided imagery, and visualization also help to manage stress. Connecting with friends and family, engaging in hobbies, listening to music, and reading a book have proven effective in managing stress. Talking to a trusted friend or a therapist is another way to help manage stress. Avoiding illicit drugs, non-prescribed prescription drugs, excessive alcohol, and excessive caffeine also helps reduce the effects of stress because such substances exacerbate the effects of stress. Too much screen time (TV, computer, video games) can also increase the effects of stress.

BENEFITS OF STRESS MANAGEMENT

Physiological benefits of stress management include increased blood flow, an ache-free body, less muscle tension, lower resting and exercise heart rate, lowered blood pressure, lowered sweat response when confronted with stress, increased concentration, lowered release of stress hormones (e.g., cortisol), and improved mood. Psychological benefits of stress management include improved mood, positive self-esteem, enhanced quality of life, positive thoughts, increased confidence in handling stressful events, lowered stress response, and reduced risk of anxiety and depression. A combination of both physiological and psychological benefits can lead to overall better health.

Common Misconceptions in Health and Fitness

Common Misconceptions Regarding Physical Activity, Exercise, and Health

A common misconception is that exercise and physical activity can ward off the ill-effects of a poor diet or poor nutrition. While physical activity and exercise can burn additional calories from high caloric diets, the negative effects of diets that are high in fat and sugar remain. Another misconception is that lifting weights (barbells, dumbbells, medicine balls) is the only way to get stronger, as one can also get strong by using bodyweight. This misconception is linked to the belief that a gym is needed for exercise, even though exercise can be done at home or outdoors. There are also gender misconceptions that include the belief that girls should not participate in strength training and boys should not participate in cardiovascular activities. Both types of activities are beneficial for all gender groups. The belief that one has to exercise for long bouts of time to be effective is also erroneous because research shows that health benefits can result from short bouts of intense activities that last for as little as seven minutes.

Misconceptions About Body Size, Physical Activity, Health, Exercise, and Diet

Two common misconceptions about body size in relation to physical activity, health, exercise, and diet are that 1) a large body size or thick frame is unfit and unhealthy and 2) a small body size or thin frame is fit and healthy. In reality, it is difficult to assess fitness and determine health simply by looking at someone. A large person can be fit, healthy, and lean, whereas a thin person can be unfit, unhealthy, and overfat. It depends on the behavior and genetics of an individual. For example, a large body or a person classified as overweight can engage in regular physical activity and eat a healthy diet and have a better fitness level and metabolic profile than a sedentary (inactive) thin person who eats poorly. A fitness assessment and medical exam (e.g., blood work) are required to determine fitness, fatness, and health. These misconceptions are attributed to the war on both childhood obesity and adult obesity, which is responsible for weight loss misconceptions, such as the effects of fad diets. Fad diets are temporary programs that usually involve the extreme restriction of one or more food groups (no carbs, no fat, one meal a day) and are designed for fast weight loss. This short-term solution is not sustaining and once the fad diet stops, the lost weight is regained, and sometimes more weight is gained than prior to starting the fad diet.

Educating Students on Healthy Lifestyle and Faulty Practices

Teaching students about nutrition and the functions of nutrients at rest and during physical activity is a strategy for combating **diet misconceptions**. Using simulations and videos that accompany the misconceptions has also proven effective. Conducting **mini-research projects** by evaluating fad diets and weight loss products gives students practical opportunities to see the effects of health and fitness misconceptions. Students can also learn how to calculate their caloric needs and shop for foods (online or in-person) that promote optimal functioning, rather than the foods and calories needed for fad diets. Illustrations of the harmful effects of certain behaviors, foods, and practices are also helpful. Students should also learn how to read food labels and ingredients lists. Contraindicated exercises and joint movements and their harmful effects should also be taught (e.g., a lat pull behind the neck can damage the neck, shoulders, and back) because the risks of some exercises supersede the benefits.

Evaluating Health and Fitness Products and Services

Quackery and False Information in Health

Quackery is exaggerated, non-scientific claims (testimonials) about the benefits or effectiveness of a product. Quackery is used to sell quick-fix solutions to health and fitness problems. Quackery products tend to use actors to sell the items or testimonials from individuals who had atypical results. The adage "it's too good to be true" is a common and accurate response to quackery. Strategies used to avoid quackery and evaluate health and fitness products include reading labels and ingredients and researching where the content originates. Health and fitness products should originate from or be supported by scientific evidence or medical experts. The Food and Drug Administration (FDA) is the evaluating agency for food, drugs, medical devices, and other substances to ensure that products are safe for Americans to consume or use. Only FDA-approved items have gone through rigorous scientific evaluation that includes thousands of trials before dissemination to the public. Some FDA products require a doctor's prescription (controlled) and some are over-the-counter (e.g., aspirin, ibuprofen). The FDA further ensures safety by continual tracking of effectiveness and side effects, and will remove substances and devices from the public if the risks outweigh the benefits. Many over-the-counter health and fitness substances are neither FDA approved nor supported by scientific research.

Evaluating Information Related to Health and Fitness Programs

One strategy to use to evaluate health and related fitness programs is to determine the reputation of the source. For example, programs developed by health and fitness agencies that are accredited to grant certifications are more reputable than programs that are not. Accredited organizations have experts from diverse fields engaged in research on the most effective practices and go through a rigorous process to become accredited. Agencies with strong health and fitness programs include the American College of Sports Medicine, the American Council on Exercise, the National Academy of Sports Medicine, and the National Strength and Conditioning Association, although there are others. Nutrition programs should also be endorsed by reputable agencies, and nutrition plans should only be prescribed by licensed nutritionists or dietitians.

Evaluating Health and Fitness Facilities and Services

Visiting several health and fitness facilities is one strategy used to evaluate and determine the best option. Things to consider during visits include evaluations of facility size; equipment, including the type, age, safety, and maintenance; the location; dates of operation; parking; the distance to travel; fitness class offerings and schedule; day care options; costs; cleanliness; showering and changing facilities; members (coed, same-sex, age, general fitness, body building, power lifting); and personnel. Personal trainers and group fitness instructors should be certified by reputable agencies and certified in first aid, CPR (cardiopulmonary resuscitation), and AED (automated external defibrillation). A serviced AED and fire extinguisher should be visible, and emergency plans posted or available.

Chapter Quiz

Ready to see how well you retained what you just read? Scan the QR code to go directly to the chapter quiz interface for this study guide. If you're using a computer, simply visit the online resources page at **mometrix.com/resources719/mtlephysed** and click the Chapter Quizzes link.

The Physical Education Program

Identifying and Addressing Various Student Needs

Identifying and Meeting All Students Needs

Assessments are used to determine if students have met, not met, or are making progress towards their objectives. The teacher needs to make sure that assessments both measure the objective and are specific. For example, a general objective is being able to perform the overhand throw; however, the elements of the overhand throw (e.g., wind-up phase, follow-through) are what should be assessed. For instance, if there are five elements or critical skill cues that make up a skill, the student would need to meet four or five of the cues to meet or exceed the objective. A student who can perform two or three of the critical skill cues may indicate that they are making progress towards meeting the objective, but performing only one or none of the cues would indicate that the student is not meeting the objectives. Based on how the student is performing, corrective feedback would be given to help the student meet the objective. If a student is already proficient with all five cues, the teacher should provide instruction to make the task more challenging (e.g., run, throw, and hit the target) to keep the student progressing and to reduce boredom and off-task behaviors.

Role of Student Choice in Physical Education

Student choice is another way to differentiate and provide equitable instruction. **Equity** is defined as providing equal opportunity, sometimes through modification, whereas **equality** is treating everyone the same regardless of individual needs. While these terms are often used interchangeably, equity is the goal during instruction because not everyone has the same needs. For example, giving each student a basketball to shoot at a 10-foot basketball goal is equality, but equity is lowering the goal for students who are much shorter than their peers (e.g., four feet tall when other peers are five feet tall and taller), which makes the distance proportional to height. Student choice has shown to motivate students to engage in physical activity settings. By offering choice, students can select activities based on their strengths. Allowing student choice also reduces embarrassment for students who are unable to perform the desired outcome. Student choice also allows students to select activities that they are comfortable with and take greater challenges if desired. During choice activities, the teacher should provide progressive activities from the beginner stage to the advanced stage as students become more proficient or comfortable moving through the tasks.

Review Video: Equality vs Equity
Visit mometrix.com/academy and enter code: 685648

Equitable Instruction Practices

Teaching practices that contribute to equitable instruction include taking an inventory of student's needs through assessment and asking students questions. Tracking teacher and student behaviors can also aid in equitable instruction to determine if there are unconscious biases. For example, a teacher might call on or help boys more than girls in a class, may discipline one ethnic group more harshly than another, or give more attention to athletes than non-athletes. Tracking teacher behaviors allows for the teacher to reflect and make changes to instruction. **Reflection** is when the teacher has an opportunity to think about the lessons and determine what went well and what needs improvement. When a teacher makes a change that benefits all students, equitable instruction can be achieved.

Designing and Implementing Instruction

Safety Considerations for Designing and Implementing Instruction

Safety practices to consider when designing and implementing instruction include a warm-up and stretching before physical activity engagement. The equipment used should be damage-free and spaced where students can move about freely. **Protective equipment** should be used to prevent injury (e.g., shin guards, helmets, weather-appropriate clothing). When instruction is outside in the heat and sun, protective clothing, hats, and sunscreen should be encouraged, and water should be easily accessible. Students should be informed of precautions to take when engaging in road activities (walking, jogging, cycling, skating). The teacher should watch for **overexertion** and carefully observe students who have a **medical condition** (e.g., asthma). An **emergency plan** should be in place and teachers should be certified in first aid and CPR or have knowledge of actions to take for common injuries in physical education. Teachers should also know when to call 911 and who will make the call in the event of an emergency.

Motivation Considerations for Design and Instruction

Teachers can create an environment where all students can succeed, which helps build student confidence in the ability to complete more difficult tasks. This is known as **self-efficacy**, which fosters intrinsic motivation. Teachers should provide positive feedback, allow for student choice, and have students set goals. The teacher can also set up the environment where students are encouraged and allowed to make mistakes by allowing multiple non-accessed opportunities to practice or engage in the activities. The teacher can design healthy competitive activities (e.g., no one is eliminated, balance ability groups for fair and equal teams, don't keep score) as some students do not enjoy competitive activities, which can demotivate students. If available, the teacher can also recommend that higher performing or competitive students enroll in sport-specific or competitive physical education courses. The teacher can give rewards (e.g., student choice, stickers, pencils), which has shown effective, although these should be used with caution because they can negatively impact intrinsic motivation, especially when not related to learning. The teacher should design lessons that allow for social interaction and provide students with a rationale (reasons, objectives) for tasks to aid motivation.

Student Progress and Physical Education

Instructional strategies that aid in ensuring students' progress include high expectations, providing adequate learning time to engage in activities, giving students maximum opportunities to respond, providing students with cues and corrective feedback (e.g., "Look up," "Keep your eyes on the ball," "Use a wider stance"), differentiation in instruction (written, oral, physical, video), and accommodating students' learning styles (verbal and auditory, visual, and kinesthetic instruction). Assessments also ensure students' progress (self, peer, formative, homework, quizzes), which should vary and appropriately address the objectives. Students can be motivated by incorporating curriculum that is developmentally appropriate (larger size equipment for students in the primary grades) and encourages student social responsibility and social skills (putting equipment away, team work). A safe, equitable, inclusive, and cooperative environment has elements that have all shown to help students improve.

Varying Instructional Approaches

There are various approaches and accompanying models used in physical education, including skill development (skill themes approach), team sports (sport education model, tactical games), and physical fitness and health-related fitness education. The skill themes approach is primarily used in elementary school and focuses on building the fundamental movement skills used in individual and dual sports. There are two common approaches when teaching team sports. The **sport education**

model is where students not only play the sport, but are also responsible for leadership roles, including coaching, refereeing, keeping score, calculating statistics, managing equipment, and other roles specific to the sport which foster team cohesion and leadership. This model provides students with details involved in all aspects involved in sports rather than focusing only on skills and game play. In contrast, the **tactical games approach** is designed to promote cognitive connections with the physical aspects of play and focuses heavily on building students' decision-making skills. Fitness education models are designed for students to engage in health-related fitness to prevent disease and increase the quality of life. Fitness curriculums are generally introduced during middle school with increased focus during high school.

Movement Education Framework

Movement education is the foundation of physical education programs and is where the direct physical application of psychomotor, cognitive, and affective domains derived, as well as the movement concepts of spatial awareness, effort, and relationships of the body. Movement education is another approach used often in elementary physical education programs and is most evident in creative movement, dance, and gymnastics curriculums. Movement education is not common in secondary schools because middle school physical education involves team sports and high school focuses on health-related fitness. However, movement concepts are evident in other models. When adopting a movement education approach, it is understood that students must have an understanding of how, what, why, and where the body moves and be able to demonstrate the fundamental movement skills in order to progress to more complex movements (manipulatives, games, and movement skills used in individual, dual, and team sports). A criticism of movement education is that it lacks structure as students are guided through activities to come to their own conclusions, but this criticism fails to recognize that student creativity is one of the strengths of movement education.

Materials and Technologies

There are many materials and technology tools that help students meet objectives and address their needs. A common tech tool is the heart rate monitor, which assesses the intensity of cardiovascular activities to ensure that students are working within their target heart rate zone. Heart rate monitors also add a safety element, as students can monitor when they are above their target heart rate zone and slow down activity accordingly. The pedometer is another technological tool that helps students track step count and meet activity or step count objectives. Other effective technologies include slideshows and videos of concepts and skills, which provide students with visual tools that support verbal instruction. Recording students on a device (iPad, smartphone) can provide students with visual feedback of their performance, and corrective feedback can be given for improvement. Written assignments (e.g., worksheets) and journals are materials that can be used to assess student learning and understanding. Posters or boards with objectives and cues can aid as reminders for students of the focus of the lesson.

Physical Education Models

Tactical Games Approach

The **tactical games approach** is a teaching model used to teach team sports. The goal is to develop the cognitive aspects of team sports that include skills, decision-making, and strategies, thus fostering understanding. There is an intentional focus on developing intrinsic motivation, which has shown to increase metacognition (the knowledge of how someone knows something). Rather than the direct teaching of skills in isolation that eventually lead to game play, the tactical games approach uses a whole-part-whole method where students play the game after an objective (such as "how to get open") has been presented. The teacher observes student behaviors to determine areas of growth. However, feedback is given in the form of questions (inquiry-based) to the group to help guide the students in solving problems. For example, the teacher might state, "I noticed that Team A had a difficult time getting open. What are some things we can do to get open?" With the teacher's guidance, students brainstorm and share techniques, then implement during the next gameplay session. Gameplay is paused for a debrief session to discuss if and how the objective was met. Students then practice the identified problems and return to play to work on implementing concepts, skills, and strategies discussed during the debriefing session.

Cooperative Learning

Cooperative learning is a teaching approach used in physical education settings. **Cooperative learning** is a student-centered, non-competitive approach that develops tasks around group work or through collaboration. Cooperative learning complements the affective domain that includes values, feelings, and sportsmanship. The fostering of collaboration (teamwork) is a strength of this approach because it requires students to work together to meet goals. This is one of many approaches that can be used to teach team sports (e.g., basketball, lacrosse), as group members share a common goal and work together to accomplish it. Using this approach alone may limit the amount of motor skill development needed to perform the skills necessary for team sports, as the learning environment is designed so students can solve problems rather than listen to the teacher explicitly provide the information.

Skill Themes Approach

The **skill themes approach** is an elementary physical education framework that aids in the development of the fundamental movement skills (locomotor, non-locomotor, and manipulative) with an overarching goal to ensure that students are proficient or competent in these areas. There are four characteristics that underpin the skill themes approach:

- Competence in the fundamental movement skills, where students are able to perform locomotor, non-locomotor, and manipulative skills, drives development.
- Providing ample student experiences to perform and develop these skills is important, as more opportunities to practice increases skill competency.
- Scope and sequence (progression) ensures that developmentally appropriate movements start from easy movements to progressively more challenging, complex movements. This is done because the more successes students have, the more likely they will be to continue to engage in physical activities. The scope and sequence characteristic focuses on stage of development rather than the age or the grade of the students.
- Instructional alignment is intentional instruction that includes objectives and assessments. Teachers explicitly plan for students to learn the fundamental movement skills by setting goals (objectives), providing activities that support the objectives, and administering ongoing assessments (formative) and cumulative final assessments (summative) to ensure students are competent in the skills or have reached mastery.

Modifying and Adapting Activities for All Students

Academic Learning Time in Physical Education

Academic learning time in physical education (ALT-PE) is a strategy used to create an equitable learning environment. ALT-PE is an observation and evaluation tool in which the teacher can analyze instructional time, student activity time in games, time off-task, learning and practice time, opportunities to respond, and equipment usage opportunities. Analysis can occur for a few students, the entire class, or an analysis of teacher behaviors to determine what is transpiring in class and to make any necessary changes. For example, the teacher may identify that a student or some students never get possession of the ball during a three vs. three basketball game. From this data, the teacher can modify the rules to require all players to touch or have possession of the ball at least three times before scoring or other parameters to ensure equal opportunity. The teacher may also observe an imbalance in teams by numbers or abilities and can modify the rules, change team rosters, or provide extra equipment to level the playing field.

Developmentally Appropriate Modifications

Game rules, equipment, and activities should be **modifiable** to ensure that all students participate, learn, and succeed. For example, beginners may be allowed to travel with a basketball when learning how to dribble as stop-and-go action limits the opportunity to practice and learn. The teacher can also use basketballs of different sizes to accommodate varying hand sizes or use balls that include the correct hand and finger-pad placements (palm print) to help guide the students with proper technique. **Developmentally appropriate game modifications** include limiting the number of rules, skills, and strategies to help build competence before more difficult tasks. Increasing the amount of balls used in team sports also creates more equity in skill development. For example, using three to five soccer balls of different colors during game play, whether with the same or different criteria for each ball (dribbling, passing, etc.), allows for more students to get involved. Targets and goals can also be positioned closer, farther, higher, wider, or narrower to accommodate various abilities.

Adaptations to Activities

Adaptations that promote equity in opportunities for students to participate, learn, and succeed include using lighter weight equipment, making goals wider and larger (for students having difficulty) or shorter and narrower (for students who need more challenge as they are proficient with the normal goals), decreasing target distances (for students unable to reach the target), allowing peers to assist students who may have physical challenges (e.g., wheelchair-bound), and including more frequent rest or water breaks for unfit or obese students. Other adaptations include how objects are manipulated to ensure equitable activity. For example, some students may be able to kick a moving ball, while others may need to kick a stationary ball or drop kick a ball. A lighter ball can also be used for students with less muscular strength (e.g., a student with muscular dystrophy or muscular atrophy). Adaptations should be student specific. For example, if one or two students need an adaptation, the entire group should not be required to engage in the adaptation, as it may not meet their needs and could possibly impede the progress of others, which can increase off-task behaviors.

Providing Appropriate and Effective Feedback

Providing Positive Feedback

Positive feedback increases student motivation and performance. Specific positive feedback is more effective than general feedback. For example, "Good job" is general feedback that does not inform the student of what went well or what was good about the performance. A more effective example is, "Good job, I like that you kept moving during the entire aerobic session. Next time, try to march in place with high knees rather than walk in place with low knees to increase your heart rate and reach your target heart rate zone. By increasing the intensity, you will increase your cardiovascular endurance, which leads to a healthy heart and better overall health." In this example, the teacher provides positive feedback on something they are doing well and provides an explicit suggestion on how to improve in this area along with its own rationale. Not all students will need corrective or improvement feedback; however, feedback is necessary to increase the challenge for students who meet or exceed the objective.

Verbal and Nonverbal Teaching Cues

Verbal and nonverbal teaching cues help with student performance. Verbal cues are descriptive words or phrases that help students perform a skill or task. Verbal cues should be short and brief (no longer than three to four words) for ease in delivery and student retention. Cues that are too long are difficult to remember and may confuse students and impede progress. Common verbal cues include "follow-through" (overhand thrown), "squish the bug" (pivot), "t-shape" (forming a "T" with the body), and "move like an airplane" (locomotor movement and speed). Teachers can make up cues designed for the student population, region, or based on the school's mascot (e.g., "Tiger high-five"). To cue (lead) a group fitness or aerobics session, verbal cues should be given in advance to give students time to respond, as there is a brief delay while the brain processes the verbal information. Nonverbal teaching cues include hand gestures (pointing in a direction, as when leading a group fitness or aerobic dance session), moving the head and eyes in different directions, facial expressions (smiling at a correct behavior or frowning when a student does something inappropriate), and thumbs up, down, and sideways can be used for cues and to provide behavioral or performative feedback. Written cues (nonverbal) posted around the gym or teaching space that support the verbal cues students refer to when needed are useful to reinforce the concepts and address the various learning styles.

Assessment in Physical Education

Types of Formal Assessments

Assessment	Advantages	Disadvantages	When to use
Observational checklists	Fast and easy (Y/N)	Non-descriptive	During large class sizes; can be used as pre-tests or post-tests.
Performance assessments	Descriptive and student-specific; allows the teacher to evaluate if students are able to put skills and concepts into practice.	Can take up a lot of time; without recording and reviewing, the teacher can miss performances.	During game or activity play; when assessing one or two concepts (e.g., getting open, shooting).
Fitness tests	Fitness tests assess health-related and skill-related fitness; fitness tests are often easy to administer; fitness tests have a competitive element, which is great for high-performing, competitive students.	Fitness tests can take up a lot of instructional time; some students may get embarrassed, especially if they are unfit, overweight, or non-competitive; fitness tests have a competitive element, which has shown to demotivate some students; shown ineffective when not connected to learning and fitness principles	To measure fitness before, during, and after instruction, practice, or training to evaluate growth and deficits and to adjust programming.

Informal Assessments

Assessment	Advantages	Disadvantages	When to use
Journals	Students can reflect and see their growth over time; there are no right or wrong answers; students can write in journals at home; students take ownership of their learning.	Writing time can take away from physical activity time; journals can be difficult to mark or assess.	At the end of each class or unit, or assigned for homework.
Peer coaching	Increases student learning opportunities, as this requires explaining, correcting, or identifying correct and incorrect performances; after students are trained, assessment time can decrease; promotes social interaction; all students get to lead (coach) and follow (receive coaching).	Reliant on students who may provide inaccurate information or do not fully understand; can take up instructional time as students have to be taught how to use it and what to look for; some students may give improper feedback (e.g., higher or lower marks because of friendship status).	Large class sizes; limited space where half the class is performing while the other half is coaching; when focusing on the affective domain.

Selecting, Constructing, Adapting, and Implementing Assessments

Standards, objectives, students' needs, class size, facilities, and equipment should all be used to select, construct, adapt, and implement assessments in physical education. Pre-assessments should occur at the beginning of a new lesson, unit, or concept to determine the ability and needs of the students, which should consist of the objectives or the desired outcome by the end of the lesson. For example, if the goal is to have students engage in 10 or 20 minutes of continuous aerobic activity, then the pre-assessment would consist of asking students to perform cardiovascular activities (jogging, team sports, step aerobics) to the best of their ability for as long as they can. Some students will complete this objective, while others may tire before the time expires. Based on these data points, the teacher will construct or design cardiovascular activities that help students reach the goal. Progress can be tracked over time. Longer rest breaks are an adaptation to accommodate students with low ability, while shorter rest breaks would accommodate students with high ability. While the cardiovascular activities should vary in class for improvement, the activity used for the assessment should be practiced regularly and used as the post-assessment.

Technology in Fitness Assessment

Heart Rate Monitors and Pedometers for Monitoring Activity Levels

Technological devices used in physical education to assess progress in fitness and performance include pedometers and heart rate monitors. These devices help the teacher and students track and analyze performance, including step count (pedometers), intensity, and duration (heart rate monitors). For example, 10,000 steps a day is a good goal to ensure that a moderate level of physical activity is achieved. Teachers and students can track and examine daily, weekly, or monthly step count to determine if students have improved, regressed, or maintained their level of activity. Steps achieved during class can also be used, and pedometers can be worn during most physical activities, not just walking or running. Tracking heart rate also aids in determining student progress in cardiovascular fitness, as engaging in consistent cardiovascular activities usually leads to lower resting heart rates. Heart rate monitors can also track when students are working too hard or not hard enough.

Activity Trackers, Fitness Applications, and Websites for Tracking Activities

In addition to heart rate monitors and pedometers, other activity trackers are found on fitness and computer applications (apps) via smartphones, tablets, devices worn on the wrist, and website platforms. When using website platforms, students can enter the types, duration, and frequency of activities that they engage in. Recommendations are given based on anthropometric measures (height, weight), gender, age, activity levels, and fitness goals. Many platforms allow for the entry of nutrition intake, which further aid in activity recommendations. Activity trackers worn around the wrist or carried on a cell phone have accelerometers which, in addition to tracking step count, measure speed and distance traveled. Many activity trackers also have the ability to measure heart rate. There are also weight training apps where students can enter the amount of weight lifted, reps, and sets. As with cardiovascular tracking, the amount of reps, sets, or weight lifted should increase over time.

Interpreting Performance Data

Cardiovascular data analysis and interpretation includes tracking resting and exercise heart rates (HR) over time, as both provide insight on health risks and improvement and should decrease over time with participation in frequent cardiovascular activities. A normal resting HR is between 60 and 90 beats per minute (bpm). Individuals who engage in regular physical activity may have resting heart rates lower than 60 bpm. For instance, if a student starts with a resting heart rate of 90 bpm, with consistent training, the resting heart rate should decrease. A resting HR over 90 bpm is considered high. Students over 90 bpm should be referred to a physician.

Muscular fitness data analysis and interpretation includes tracking the amount of weight lifted and the number of repetitions over time. The weight and reps should increase, which illustrates growth and improvement. For example, if a student went from lifting 3 sets of 8 pounds at 10 repetitions at the beginning of the semester to lifting 3 sets of 15 pounds at 10 repetitions, that indicates an improvement in strength. However, going from lifting 3 sets of 8 pounds at 10 repetitions to lifting 3 sets of 8 pounds at 20 repetitions indicates an improvement in muscular endurance, and the student will likely need to increase the weight for greater improvement and challenge.

Fitness Feedback and Recommendations for Students

Fitness feedback is often given in the form of a recommendation or suggestion. For all types of feedback, it is helpful to start with a positive comment on what the student is doing well. For example, "I love that you are trying this out!" Next, state the issue: "I noticed that you are just below your target heart rate zone." Instead of directly giving the student the answers, ask students questions that can help guide them to an appropriate answer while also checking for understanding: "What can you do to increase your exercise heart rate?" Pause for student responses. If they are accurate, support and commend their response. The teacher can also make a few suggestions: "Try to engage or move your arms," or "Incorporate high-impact movements and take larger steps." Students who do not challenge themselves or who have not grasped fitness concepts may be encouraged to choose a heavier weight (intensity), conduct more repetitions (duration), engage in physical activity an additional day or two each week (frequency), or find an activity they enjoy (sport, hiking).

Cultural Influences on Student Physical Activity

Effects of Peer Pressure and Media Messages

The media has a strong influence on children and adolescents and can positively or negatively impact students' attitudes regarding engagement in physical activity. The same is true for pressure from peers, which is especially strong during adolescence. Media messages and images tend to focus on thinness and unhealthy methods to achieve it, including extreme calorie restriction and extreme exercising. Awareness of these factors have improved and include positive messages from the National Football League (NFL) to "Play 60," which encourages children to engage in 60 minutes of physical activity every day. Positive and negative peer pressure also impact student attitudes and engagement in physical activity. For example, peers who value and appreciate physical activity can sometimes convince friends to engage in physical activity. In contrast, peers who do not value and appreciate physical activity can undermine positive messages given by the teacher and influence classmates not to engage.

Effects of Cultural Influences

Culture, family background, and community all influence student attitudes on physical activity engagement. For example, if a student is in a family that does not value physical activity, they may adopt those same beliefs and vice versa. Sometimes families do value physical activity, but they may not have the privilege of leisure time to engage in physical activity because they may work long hours, have an additional job or jobs, or have childcare responsibilities. Some families and communities are unaware of the benefits of physical activity. Furthermore, there are some cultures and religions that are not keen on physical activity, especially for girls and women, which will influence students' attitudes and engagement in physical activity. To combat some of the negative messages surrounding physical activity that some students may receive at home, share the benefits of physical activity with parents by inviting them to school events, creating family fun activity nights or weekends, or sending emails or newsletters with tips for improving health and exercise to keep them informed and engaged. It may possibly change their negative perceptions of physical activity engagement.

Gender Expectations in Physical Education

Title IX, introduced in 1972, provides equal access to physical activity and sports to female students. Prior to its introduction, girls were more culturally discouraged from engaging in vigorous physical activities which were considered less feminine. Instead, females who wanted to participate in athletics usually only had options in activities such as dance and gymnastics and were steered away from team sports. While more female students participate in sports today, there are still differences in cultural expectations for males and females. Females tend to have lower expectations to participate in competitive athletics, whereas males are generally expected to participate as a rite of passage into manhood. This distinction can act as a cultural gender stereotype that leads to unhealthy habits or tends to exclude students who want to participate in sports or force students to engage in activities to a higher degree than is reasonable to expect.

Effects of Body Image Expectations

Body image and skill level both have a powerful impact on student attitudes and engagement in physical activity. Students who are highly skilled tend to enjoy physical education and physical activity, whereas low-skilled students have less enjoyment. Negative concepts of body image also impact attitudes and engagement in physical activity. When students do not feel good about their bodies, they are less likely to engage in physical activity due to a fear of being judged for their appearance. This fear is common among obese students. Alternatively, students may suffer from anorexia nervosa, an eating and mental disorder where one starves themselves because of an irrational fear of gaining weight, and may engage in extreme and unhealthy levels of physical activity.

Student Motivation and Lifelong Physical Fitness

Motivating Students to Participate in Lifelong Physical Activity

Teachers who role model or engage in physical activity have shown to motivate students to engage in physical activity for life. Students who are skilled or proficient in the fundamental movement patterns are also more likely to engage in physical activities as adults. Positive feedback with explicit acknowledgement of effort and improvement is another effective strategy that encourages regular physical activity. Furthermore, activities that promote self-efficacy and autonomy, which are better achieved with student goal-setting, also help foster physical activity engagement. Students who have knowledge of the benefits of physical activity and the consequences of not engaging in physical activity further foster motivation to engage in physical activity over the lifespan.

Effects of Self-Assessment and Progress Tracking on Student Motivation

Self-assessment aids in motivating students to participate in lifelong physical activity as it allows students to evaluate their own performance. From the assessment, students evaluate and reflect on their performance and will either continue, revise, or update goals. As students revisit goals and create a plan to achieve those goals, they will track progress over time to determine growth or the lack thereof. Ongoing self-assessment and reflection allows students to take ownership and responsibility in their performance and develop a plan suitable for their needs. These activities help develop intrinsic motivation, which has shown more effective than extrinsic motivation in promoting lifelong physical activity.

Self-Efficacy

Self-efficacy is belief in one's ability to perform motor skills. The development of self-efficacy leads to self-motivation and is strongly associated with engaging in physical activity over the lifespan. There are four circumstances that have shown to increase self-efficacy listed below.

- Past performance: previous experience of accomplishment or success in a performance task or skill (success in one sport increases the self-efficacy of learning a new sport)
- Observing others (vicarious learning): watching someone else perform the task or exhibit the skill, which fosters confidence to attempt and perform the task or develop the ("If they can do it, so can I")

- Verbal persuasion: encouragement from a teacher, parent, or peer ("You can do it!")
- Physiological cues: kinesthetic responses to the environment (body position or sensory awareness, which is enhanced through repetition and practice)

Classroom and Resource Management

Organizing Time, Location, and Equipment

Planning ahead and providing clear and concise instructions will reduce classroom management and behavioral issues. A schedule of teaching space should be known long before the semester begins. Once the location has been determined, the dimensions of the space and knowledge of the type, amount, and location of equipment should also be known. If there are other teachers on staff, communication on teaching rotations and activities should be discussed to avoid conflicts and time wasting. Establishing routines from student entry and exit, attendance, warm-up, equipment distribution, and equipment cleanup helps students move quickly without losing instructional time or allowing time for students to get off task. A strategy for entrance and attendance is to have students walk to assigned squad lines and conduct an active warm-up while attendance is taken. The teacher can take attendance or assign a squad line leader. Squad lines make it easy to see who is absent. Another management strategy is to post instructions for an instant activity (IA) that can be conducted as soon as students enter the field or gym. Attendance should be taken during the IA, which allows students to immediately engage and reduces time for off-task behaviors. This IA can also serve as a warm-up or an opportunity to pre-assess or post-assess students' skill levels and performance.

Allocating Time, Location, and Equipment

Every minute of instructional time should be accounted for. All tasks and activities, including transitions, should have an allotted time when lesson planning (e.g., three minutes, five minutes). The equipment should be out and ready for easy retrieval (e.g., on the sidelines, in the corners of the teaching space). If outside, a backup plan (go to the gym, multi-purpose room, or classroom) should be in place in case of inclement or unsafe weather (e.g., rain, heat, cold). Students should be trained and assigned roles to help put equipment away. This saves time and promotes personal responsibility and teamwork, which will minimize disruptions in the future. When sharing teaching space, communication and planning are extremely important because conflicts are likely to occur when there is a communication breakdown. Teachers who teach at the same time, in the same place, and use the same equipment should meet before the school year to map out activities, equipment usage (setting up and breaking down), teaching space (one-half or one-third of the court or field), rules, routines, duties, and protocols (e.g., locker room, attendance, and warm-up procedures) to optimize the learning experience. Some teachers elect to team teach, where one teacher leads while the other helps facilitate. This is often done so teachers can teach to their strengths and to reduce management issues.

Review Video: Creating Effective Lesson Plans
Visit mometrix.com/academy and enter code: 100377

Classroom Management Approaches

Large class sizes, minimal space, and lack of equipment are limitations of taking attendance, physical activities, and managing time. Large classes require more time to move and take attendance, and they require extra safety measures in cramped spaces. Squad lines (students arranged in rows or lines of 5–10 students, forming a box shape) are more effective than instant activities for large groups because students are more contained, which reduces the risk of injury.

Large class sizes, minimal space, and the lack of equipment do not give students the opportunity to engage in all of the same activities at the same time. For example, a common approach is to have half of the class in the center of the court or field engaging in activities, while the other half are doing activities on the sidelines. While this approach increases safety, it does not allow students to fully engage in the learning objectives and decreases practice time for refinement and improvement. Large class sizes also make it more difficult for the teacher to see all students and provide appropriate feedback.

Review Video: Classroom Management - Rhythms of Teaching
Visit mometrix.com/academy and enter code: 809399

Maintaining a Positive Learning Climate

Gender Diverse Classes

To avoid gender favoritism and gender disparities in physical education, teachers should expect all students to engage in the activities and work towards the performance goals. Teachers should create coeducational activities and incorporate student preferences into the curriculum and activities. All students should be included in activities and games regardless of gender stereotypes (e.g., boys engaging in dance and gymnastics and girls engaging in team sports like football). Teachers should not use or allow stereotypic language like, "You throw like a girl." The teacher should also monitor time given to all groups to ensure equal time is given and that one group does not dominate another. The teacher can also reflect on their behaviors to make sure that they are not responding to one gender group over another.

Mixed-Ability Classes

A cooperative environment helps foster inclusion in mixed ability classes. Depending on the objective, groups can contain students of mixed abilities, but sometimes students with the same abilities need to be grouped. For example, novice learners may need to be grouped together to focus on skill levels because grouping these novices with more skilled students may intimidate and discourage them from participation. The skilled students may get frustrated as beginner skills and activities below their more advanced skill level become boring and causes them to go off task. However, sometimes mixed groupings may be beneficial when peer coaching or teaching is practiced and advanced students work with beginners, since there is evidence that students learn best from peers.

Different Cultural Backgrounds

Strategies that promote a healthy social climate for students of various cultural backgrounds include offering diverse curricula, activities, and teaching approaches that include all student groups. If English is a second or additional language for students, cues and assignments should also include the student's first language. Respect and understanding of other cultures should be the standard, and derogatory language and behaviors should not be tolerated. The teacher should explore cultural practices, differences in discipline, and physical activity expectations. For instance, in some cultures, it is disrespectful to look teachers or authority figures in the eyes. In other cultures, and in some religions, physical activity is discouraged. In these instances, asking questions about cultural and physical activity expectations and conveying the facts (not opinions) about the benefits of physical activity and social engagement in American culture should be shared with students and parents. Additionally, some cultures and religions do not allow for bare skin to be exposed, so students should not be penalized if these factors prevent them from changing out of their clothing and into the school PE uniform.

Developing Positive Interpersonal Skills in Physical Education

Developing Confidence through Physical Activities

Games and sports promote the development of confidence through leadership in both the various roles involved and accomplishing a goal. For example, in team sports, everyone has a role and a responsibility that helps the team work towards a goal. Games and sports also involve competition, which provides opportunities to develop competence, which has shown to increase motivation and confidence. Successful students, players, and teams tend to have greater confidence than unsuccessful students, players, and teams. Therefore, the learning environment should be challenging yet attainable to help build confidence. Dance helps promote confidence as students are able to move freely without judgment or competition. In dances that involve steps, learning or mastery of these dances helps build confidence through accomplishing the task of learning the dance steps.

Fairness and Respect for Diversity

Games and sports are governed by rules that involve fair play. Fair play has to be taught and includes personal responsibility, showing respect to self and others, giving full effort, and being helpful. Diversity is promoted through games and sports as teams and opponents tend to include different types of individuals (gender, race, ethnicity, ability, learning styles), and sport and games allow for interactions across groups that can aid in a better understanding of similarities and differences. A respect for diversity can also be developed and promoted through dance as individuals have the opportunity to engage in freedom of expression. In PE curricula, dances from around the world and from different cultures are taught (the Virginia reel, polka, African dance, folk dances, square dance), exposing children to other people's cultures and fostering inclusion, diversity, and respect for others.

Conflict Resolution Skills

Outdoor pursuits help develop conflict resolutions skills by having students engage in challenging tasks like high ropes courses and partner or group activities like trust falls. Partner and group activities require frequent communication to problem solve or accomplish a task. Dual and team sports are also avenues that promote conflict resolution skills, as communication is needed for the team's success. It is customary for a player to apologize when they make an error. Players also communicate how to strategize against an opponent, which is an example of solving a problem. For example, when a teammate keeps losing to his or her opponent, the team will need to communicate with each other to either switch roles, provide assistance, or utilize a different defensive strategy to solve the problem.

Turn Taking and Teamwork

Games and sports require cooperation and collaboration, thus promoting teamwork. Teamwork is shown through working together to score a point, playing defense and offense, and communicating to accomplish these tasks. Taking turns is evident in games and sports when players have to substitute in and out of a game. In softball and baseball, batters have to wait for their turn. Taking turns is also evident in group games like jumping rope, where the jumpers have to wait for the person in front to complete their jump before entering. The rope turners also take turns. Students or players on the sidelines also demonstrate teamwork by cheering and encouraging other active students or players.

Treating Opponents with Respect and Leadership Skills

Promoting sport and game etiquette teaches how players should treat their opponents. For example, if a player from the opposing team falls, a respectful act would be to assist the opponent with getting up. During a sport, it is common to take a knee out of respect when a player gets injured. This knee position is held until the player gets up or is taken off of the field or court. Calling personal fouls and apologizing if one causes harm are other examples of treating opponents with respect that are developed and promoted through games and sports. Wishing the opposition good luck before the game and shaking hands at the end of play are other examples of how to treat opponents with respect. Opportunities for leadership are shown in roles including team captain and the positions played. For example, in basketball, the point guard is usually responsible for bringing the ball up the court and calling the offense, making this player the leader in this capacity. Other players also have a role and lead in their respective positions.

Examples of Leadership, Taking Turns, and Loyalty in Outdoor Activities

Examples of teamwork, taking turns, and loyalty are evident in outdoor activities. For instance, rock climbing activities in physical education require a climber and three to four belayers (anchors who support the climber). The belayers work and communicate as one unit and provide safety (loyalty) and leadership for the climber. The belayers also provide encouragement to help the climber reach the top of the climb, which illustrates leadership. If the belayers are not focused while supporting the climber, injury can occur. Climbers and belayers change roles, which illustrates taking turns. In partner or couples' dances (foxtrot, tango, salsa), there is a leader and follower, which gives students opportunities to engage in leadership. These roles are usually switched back and forth, which illustrates taking turns in the leader and follower roles. The climber in rock climbing and the follower in dance have to trust that the belayers and leader know what they are doing, and consistency in performance helps students demonstrate loyalty.

Promoting Self-Management Skills

Self-monitoring refers to observations of self, when a student tries to pay close attention to what he or she is doing while they perform. **Self-assessment** is slightly different and refers to a reflective process in which students try to grade their performance to look for room for improvement. Self-assessment is slightly more formal and can be done after the activity is complete. Both are used to help students reflect on and evaluate their own performance by identifying strengths, weaknesses, and the learning process. These self-monitoring methods are self-regulation strategies or self-management skills that help students take ownership of their learning. Self-management skills include the ability to identify successes and failures and to create goals for improvement, which promotes intrinsic motivation to engage in physical activity. Of these strategies, goal setting is considered the most important because students are choosing their own specific focus and outcome. As such, goals should be specific and measurable, which helps students determine the next steps for practice, remediation, or growth.

Student Responsibility and Self-Control

Assigning roles to students helps them develop responsible behaviors and self-control. Common roles in physical education include line or squad line leader, exercise or warm-up leader, equipment manager, and attendance taker. Behavioral rules and expectations help promote self-control. A common behavioral method used in physical education is Don Hellison's teaching personal and social responsibility (TPSR) model, which aims to teach personal and social responsibility. The TPSR model has five levels listed below.

- Respect for others' rights and feelings: manage temper, work towards peaceful conflict resolution
- Effort: practice and learn persistence and intrinsic motivation, take on challenges
- Self-direction: goal-setting, refraining from peer pressure

- Helping others
- Behaviors are carried over outside of the gym: the goal of having values learned in class transfer to other environments (e.g., home, playground)

These behaviors can be the focus during an individual lesson, unit, or every lesson. However, students are often taught each level and evaluate where they were on a particular day or lesson. It is recommended that this model is embedded with other instructional models because stand-alone use is not effective for behavior change.

Hellison's Teaching Personal and Social Responsibility (TPSR) Model

Hellison's **Teaching Personal and Social Responsibility** (TPSR) model seeks to promote students' ability to take responsibility for their actions in the physical education classroom and carry that responsibility into the students' lives. This model, therefore, is useful in helping to develop students' ability to **manage success** and **failure** well. The elements of the TPSR model apply to both success and failure. Students who may care too much about winning or losing may lose their temper when losing, and therefore may need to work on improving their **respect** for others' rights and feelings. Other students may not care enough about success and may not put in the necessary **effort** to perform well. Alternatively, a student who succeeds in sports on talent may have a poor attitude about their abilities and not respect other students who are not as skilled. Another consequence might be that a talented student may not put forth the effort required to further develop their skills. The **self-direction** stage may be a good focal point for a student who remains unchallenged without specific goals. Helping the student to **self-evaluate** and target particular skills may help to keep the student motivated and able to grow more efficiently. Ultimately, the goals of TPSR are skills well suited to learning through physical education, but apply to the whole life of a student.

Students' Goal-Setting Abilities

To help students develop goal-setting abilities, they must be taught that goals should be specific and measurable. An example should be given, such as, "I can hit the target 6 out of 10 times." Students should be told to create a moderately challenging goal. A goal that is too easy lacks challenge, and a goal that is too difficult can create frustration. Students should also be encouraged to set short-term and long-term goals. When students set their own goals, they gain a sense of accomplishment and personal satisfaction, which fosters intrinsic motivation and competence.

Problem-Solving Skills

Teachers can help students analyze and problem-solve through guided discovery and cooperative learning. **Guided discovery** is when the teacher structures the environment to where students can figure out or solve the problem on their own. Using this method, the teacher asks students questions to help "guide" them to accomplish predetermined tasks. This has also been called a **problem-solving approach.** Rather than having one right answer, there are usually several options to complete the tasks. For example, a task may be to get from one obstacle to another without walking. Students would then analyze the obstacles, make a decision on what they think is the best method, and attempt the tasks. If the students are successful, they have solved the problem. To further aid in analyzing and problem-solving, the teacher may follow up and ask if there is another way to complete the task, at which time students would have to continue with their analysis and attempt to solve the problem another way.

Decision-Making Skills

Tactical learning approaches help students with decision-making skills used in individual, dual, and team sports. In sports, every move made or action performed is a decision. Practicing sports skills during modified game play (e.g., the tactical approach) allows students opportunities to consistently make decisions. Depending on the outcome of the decision, students will either continue or, if the outcome is negative, do something different. For example, if a student conducted a fake before kicking the ball into the goal, he or she may try to do the same thing the next time. However, if the fake was unsuccessful and the ball got stolen, the student will likely make a different choice. If a student continues to make the same error, the teacher may have to ask questions to help the student do something different. Experiencing various tactics helps students develop an inventory of things to do and what decision to make according to the environment.

Goals, Trends, and Philosophies of Physical Education Programs

Purpose of Physical Education Programs

The main purpose of physical education programs is to ensure that students are physically literate. According to the Society of Health and Physical Educators of America (SHAPE), **physical literacy** is "the ability to move with competence and confidence in a wide variety of physical activities in multiple environments that benefit the healthy development of the whole person." With the goal of physical literacy, physical education programs are designed to promote physical activity over the lifespan. To do this, quality physical education programs ensure that students are engaged in psychomotor (movement), cognitive (thinking), and affective (social and emotional) domains, thus influencing the development of the whole person.

Role of the Society of Health and Physical Educators of America (SHAPE)

SHAPE America is the oldest and largest physical education professional organization in the United States. SHAPE is the national governing body of physical education, and each state and US territory has a SHAPE (a.k.a. AAHPERD) equivalent (e.g., Texas Association for Health, Physical Education, Recreation and Dance, or TAHPERD). There are five SHAPE districts which combine states and territories by region. For example, TAHPERD is in the Southern District along with 12 other states. SHAPE America sets the national physical education standards and learning outcomes; however, each state can decide whether to adopt SHAPE standards, devise their own, or use a combination of SHAPE and state-level standards. For example, Texas has its own standards called the Texas Essential Knowledge and Skills (TEKS). SHAPE America and state-level organizations require membership, but both advocate for physical education, disseminate best teaching practice information, provide professional development, and manage state and national policies—usually for free. They also hold annual conferences where teachers and experts hold teaching workshops and training.

State-Level Physical Education Programs

Physical education programs in each state and US territory are governed by state-level law and policy. These laws and policies include setting physical education requirements that concern the format (in-class or online), amount, and frequency of physical education; the time allocated for physical education; and fitness testing, teacher certification requirements, and class size. These are usually minimums or recommendations that school districts should aim to achieve. For example, the state of Texas requires that students in elementary school engage in structured physical activity for at least 135 minutes every week, and at least 30 minutes a day for students in middle school. High school students must earn 1.0 physical education credit, but each school district determines the implementation. The state also decides on waivers, exemptions (Texas does not allow for waivers and exemptions), and activities that can be substituted for physical education (e.g., athletic sports team participation, JROTC, dance teams).

Local School District Physical Education Programs

While the state sets physical education standards and determines the number of minutes students should be actively engaged in elementary and middle schools, schools have flexibility in the structure of the physical education program. For instance, schools are responsible for scheduling, teaching models and modalities, class size, and curriculum approaches. For example, the state of Texas requires a maximum of 45:1 student-teacher ratio in physical education, however, districts and schools may choose to endorse SHAPE America's 25:1 student-teacher ratio for elementary grades, 30:1 for middle school grades, and 35:1 for high school grades. Some states do not require physical education teacher certification for school districts, but most public school districts require a degree in physical education and physical education teacher certification. Private and parochial schools are governed independently and do not have to adhere to district policies.

Trends in Physical Education

Due to an increase in childhood obesity related to poor dietary habits and sedentary lifestyles, many physical education programs have shifted to health-related fitness curriculums instead of team sport curriculums in efforts to prevent obesity. Fitness and physical activity have also shown to improve brain functioning and learning. This is especially true in high school, when students are preparing for adulthood and making independent choices. Many schools now have fitness centers and weight rooms to meet the needs of this trend. Technology is used to monitor fitness, including heart rate monitors, pedometers, and activity trackers. Another trend is the focus on social and emotional learning (SEL) due to increased mental health concerns of youth and the understanding that physical education and physical activity can aid in reducing and managing mental health risks. As a result, there has been an increase in yoga and mindfulness in physical education programs.

Common Issues in Physical Education

Common issues that affect physical education programs are financial cuts, large class sizes, little or reduced instructional time, and the perceived lack of value in its role of educating and developing the whole child. Other issues include the lack of equipment or teaching space and frequent, unexpected teaching interruptions (e.g., the gym is needed for an assembly). Assessment and grading are also topics of debate in physical education programs, as some believe students should get an A grade for participation while others believe that students should meet learning outcomes. Fitness testing has been and continues to be an issue in physical education, especially when used for a grade. While fitness testing can be a good assessment tool and provide educational and motivational opportunities, fitness testing takes time and may embarrass some students. Other issues with fitness testing are that students are often unaware of the rationale or that they are not working on the fitness measures throughout the year.

Behaviorism, Cognitivism, and Constructivism Philosophies

Behaviorism takes on a repetitive approach. Teachers who engage in behaviorist practices focus on repetition of the ideal movement, or gold standard. The goal is to have students repeat tasks until they achieve mastery. This approach is best used for students who need more direction, as it could demotivate high-performing students. Cognitivism was developed out of disagreement with behaviorism, as the cognitive domain is not addressed. The beliefs that underpin **cognitivism** are that students will be unable to master movement without an understanding of the movement, therefore, emphasis needs to include both cognitive and psychomotor domains. As such, information processing must occur in the brain before movement can occur. **Constructivism** evolved out of cognitivism and is evident in physical education programs as constructivists believe in getting students actively involved during the learning process. For example, students who engage in and learn the history of dance will better understand movement concepts. Constructivism includes the psychomotor, cognitive, and affective domains and takes on an interdisciplinary approach. As such, students learn the skills for a game (e.g., lacrosse), the rules, the history, and the values of the game.

Humanism Philosophy

Constructivism underpins **humanism**, which focuses on the affective and cognitive domains, takes a student-centered and holistic approach, and was derived out of criticisms of behaviorism and cognitivism. Teachers who operate from a humanist framework believe in the facilitation of learning by creating optimal learning environments. These teachers provide constant encouragement and positive feedback with the aim to help students grow at their own pace and in their own time. These teachers also focus on the good (effort, persistence) of students rather than the bad (use of profane language, pushing or shoving), and try to foster the positive aspects of students. Abraham Maslow and Carl Rogers were well-known humanists who created Maslow's hierarchy of needs, which posits that when the basic needs are met (physiological, safety, belongingness, and esteem), then self-fulfillment, or self-actualization, can be achieved.

Characteristics of Effective Physical Education Programs

An effective physical education program is student-centered and attempts to balance short-term goals with lifelong health and fitness. The ultimate outcome of a physical education program is to help students fully develop their motor skills, to inform them about health and fitness principles, and help them to develop the skills to make good decisions for themselves as they transition to adulthood. The use of high expectations and standards-based instruction helps to keep students in a mode of progress toward particular goals that are generally developmentally appropriate. Instruction needs to be appropriate to the developmental needs and skill level of students. This means that classes should be appropriately sized to set specific enough goals to be effective for the class. Instruction should be rich and engaging, with adequate equipment and resources, and plenty of opportunity for extracurricular activities that will help with achieving health and fitness outcomes. With younger children, goals should be focused on developing motor skills and coordination, and as they age, they should be given more decision-making opportunity to help students take their health into their own hands as they progress from children to adults.

Purpose of Assessment and Physical Education Programming

The purposes of assessment are to determine or measure student learning and to identify strengths and deficiencies or areas of weakness. Assessment results should inform the teacher (as well as students and parents) on the next steps for improvement or growth. Psychomotor, cognitive, and affective assessments are included in effective physical education programs. The teacher should be clear in the expectations, and criteria should be communicated to students prior to assessments. The teacher should also engage in appropriate uses of physical activity and fitness assessment tools. For example, when assessing fitness, results should only be shared with students and parents, not posted on walls for all to see. Assessments should be ongoing (formative) and allow for students to self-assess and engage in monitoring their activities before a final (summative) assessment is given. There should also be adequate opportunities to respond in order to foster growth and learning.

Presidential Youth Fitness Program

The Presidential Youth Fitness Program (PYFP) is the national fitness test program designed by the United States government. The PYFP adopted FitnessGram testing protocols for its fitness assessments. FitnessGram is a battery of fitness tests designed for students aged 8–17 that measures the five health-related fitness components. These assessments are designed to assess a student's fitness to inform the teacher, student, and parents of fitness levels, strengths, areas of growth, and potential health risks. Fitness outcomes should also inform teachers how to proceed with the physical education program to ensure that meaningful fitness activities and concepts are embedded in the physical education program to help students gain knowledge and understanding of fitness principles to engage in for a lifetime. Fitness assessments should be conducted at regular intervals (e.g., every two, four, and six weeks) to monitor progress and the effectiveness of fitness programming, as these are components that reinforce effective physical education practices.

SHAPE America's Health Moves Minds

SHAPE America's Health Moves Minds is a national service-learning program that promotes the benefits of physical activity and mindfulness on overall health with a particular focus on mental health, including anxiety (extreme and exhaustive worry that affects mental and physical health) and clinical depression (mood disorder with chronic feelings of sadness). Childhood stress, anxiety, and depression are on the rise, and this program recognizes the relationship of physical activity and health. The program supports and reinforces the physical literacy concept of developing the whole child, which includes the mental, physical, emotional, and social wellbeing of students. Health Moves Minds lesson plans have been created for teachers to implement in K-12 health and physical education programs.

Evaluating the Effectiveness of the Physical Education Program

One technique used to evaluate the effectiveness of the physical education program through data collection is to track students' progress over time. For example, a student's sets, weights, and reps can be tracked to determine if strength or endurance have improved, regressed, or remained the same. The teacher and student can devise a plan (increase weight, sets, reps) to accommodate each scenario. Heart rate data can also be tracked randomly (monitor one class to see if students are working in their target heart rate) or over time to track trends in fitness. For example, taking the resting heart at the beginning, middle, and end of the semester will inform the teacher and student of intensity levels and allow them to make adjustments accordingly. Taking heart rate over time will also determine the effectiveness of the program, as the resting and exercise heart rate should stay the same or decrease. Students' oral and written responses to quizzes and tests also provide data on what is known, what is unknown, and what needs to be re-taught.

Reflecting on Teaching Practices to Shape Future Instruction

Reflective teaching helps teachers make decisions that are instructionally and developmentally appropriate. Reflective teachers take inventory (in the form of data) of their own behaviors and of students' strengths, abilities, attitudes, and deficiencies. For example, if the teacher is taking too long to give instructions, he or she can work on giving concise instruction or different delivery methods (e.g., posted on the wall, slideshow, verbal instructions). If students are kept waiting too long, the teacher may need to increase the number of stations, distribute more pieces of equipment, or reduce group sizes. If students have difficulty performing a task, the teacher should provide modifications to help the students achieve the goals. For example, if students' balls consistently hit the net during serves (tennis or volleyball), the teacher can lower the net, provide cues (toss the ball higher, make contact here), or move students closer to the net.

Reflecting on Student Assessment Data to Shape Future Instruction

Student assessment data helps the teacher determine if class activities are aligned with assessments. Assessment data also informs the teacher if assessments are too easy, just right, or too difficult. For example, if the majority of students are unable to meet the objective, then the assessment is either too difficult, inappropriate, or the activities that the teacher designed did not correspond to the assessment. Based on these data points, the teacher can reteach using different methods and activities, provide students with more time to engage in the activities, focus on different skill cues, and create a new assessment that is aligned to the activities taught. If all of the students meet the objective, then the teacher may be extremely effective or they may be administering an assessment that is too easy. In this situation, the teacher can add challenge to help students continuously improve and to increase motivation.

> **Review Video: Assessment Reliability and Validity**
> Visit mometrix.com/academy and enter code: 424680

Advocating for Physical Education

The Every Student Succeeds Act (ESSA) recognizes that health and physical education are integral parts of developing the whole child. Teachers can advocate for schools and communities by applying for state and federal support (funding) to provide quality programming in schools, including school improvement and teacher effectiveness. SHAPE America also has advocacy toolkits for physical education that includes participating in legislation events that have an impact on physical education policies and practices. Fundraising for program needs is another way to advocate for quality physical education programming. Inviting parents, school leaders, and decision-making personnel to observe physical classes is additional way to support physical education within the community.

Opportunities and Resources for Physical Activity in the School Community

Additional opportunities for physical health in schools include after-school physical activity programs, intramural and athletic teams, recess, and physical activity breaks. Some schools have fitness centers, weight rooms, swimming pools, tennis courts, and athletic fields that are open to parents and the greater school community. Information newsletters, flyers, and emails can be created and distributed to notify recipients of opportunities, as well as any specials or discounts. Making PA announcements and networking with the PTA, PTO, and PTSO (parent-teacher association, parent-teacher organization, and parent-teacher-student organization) to organize presentations for parents and the community can also help communicate this information. Teachers can also take students on field trips to local fitness centers, rock climbing walls, and other facilities that offer physical activity opportunities.

Physical Activity Opportunities and Resources in the Community

Local parks, Frisbee and disc golf parks, recreation centers, hiking trails, golf courses, fitness centers, roller skating rinks, bowling alleys, biking trails, skateboard parks, and swimming pools are additional opportunities for individuals to engage in physical activities. There are also physical activity meet-up groups that are free or have minimal costs (e.g., walking and running groups, tennis groups) where people can build community with others who enjoy similar activities. Most parks have walking or biking trails, and many have playground and exercise equipment. Recreation centers tend to offer team sporting activities (basketball, soccer, volleyball), swimming, group fitness classes, weight rooms, rock climbing, racquetball, and recreational games (shuffleboard, croquet).

Physical Education and the General Curriculum

Relationship Between Physical Education and the General Curriculum

The **integrated physical education model** incorporates other subject areas to aid in the understanding of concepts in a real-world setting and their application. Also known as **interdisciplinary learning** or an **interdisciplinary teaching model**, this model builds on how physical education is inherently aligned to other subject areas. For example, physical education teachers use and teach the principles of physics and biomechanics when teaching throwing, jumping skills, and most other physical activities. History is also taught in physical education when students learn about physical activity, sports, dance, and gymnastics history during the physical components of these activities. Robin J. Fogarty asserts that physical education is the leading field of integration and has identified the following four integration methods:

- Sequenced integration, where two or more subject areas focus on one topic
- Shared integration, or the overlap of subject areas
- Webbed integration, the use of themes to guide instruction
- Threaded integration, which combines cognitive and social domains in every subject area

Physical Education Concepts Across the Curriculum

Physical education teachers often collaborate with teachers in other subjects to determine the best approaches to meet students' needs. Sometimes physical education teachers are required to integrate by school districts or personnel. For example, some schools have DEAR (Drop Everything and Read) programs to help foster literacy and reading comprehension. Physical education teachers can select books that are related to physical education but are categorized under another subject area. Some schools choose a book or movie to integrate across all subjects and grade levels. For example, Harry Potter, the popular book and movie series, has been used in schools to teach literacy, history, math, science, art, choir, and physical education. In fact, a physical education teacher implemented the game of Quidditch from Harry Potter into his classes in response to a school's interdisciplinary approach to Harry Potter. Quidditch has become a competitive, sanctioned sport played in many physical education programs and on several college campuses.

Integrating Physical Education Concepts in Other Subject Areas

Physical education teachers can take the initiative and contact teachers in other disciplines to explore ways to incorporate physical education in other subject areas. For example, English language arts teachers can use physical education objectives to teach nouns and verb tenses. Math teachers can have students compute and analyze sports data or use sports and physical activity examples in word problems. Science teachers can incorporate exercise physiology to teach human physiology concepts or develop sporting examples to use in biomechanics. History teachers can incorporate the history of sports and physical activity, especially during events like the Olympics.

Legal and Ethical Responsibilities

Confidentiality Issues in Physical Education

There are certain legal and ethical considerations in regard to keeping student confidentiality. Any information shared in meetings about students, including students with individualized education plans (IEP) and medical or health conditions, should be kept confidential. When students share confidential information with a teacher, the teacher must weigh the risk involved and report any information a student tells them that may cause physical harm to the student or another person. For example, if a student is homicidal or suicidal, the teacher must report this immediately to the counselor and an administrator. If a student shares that they are harming themselves (e.g., cutting), this too must be shared with the counselor. However, the teacher should both encourage the student to tell the counselor themselves and inform the student of their intentions. Teachers must adhere to any school and district policies and also to local and state laws. If the student discusses a sexuality issue (gay, lesbian, transgender), pregnancy, or relationship status in confidence, disclosing this type of information, while not illegal, may eliminate student trust and could possibly pose physical or psychological harm to the student, depending on the environment.

Review Video: IEPs
Visit mometrix.com/academy and enter code: 153484

Supervision, Liability, and Neglect

Providing a safe environment is a top priority for teachers. To keep the environment safe, adequate supervision is essential. The teacher should position themselves where they can see all students and be aware of unsafe behaviors. The teacher should also be first to arrive in the teaching space, and should put rules in place if students arrive first. For instance, students should not touch any equipment or engage in physical activity until the teacher arrives and provides instructions. The teacher should check the equipment for damage, and review safety rules and post written copies in a visible, known location. Teachers should be aware of their students' strengths and limitations to ensure that activities are safe and appropriate. Accidents and injury are more frequent in physical education settings than other subject areas, thus prevention is critical so that teachers are less likely to be held liable or deemed negligent. **Liability** is a violation of responsibilities (a.k.a. duty) usually attributed to negligence. **Negligence** is misconduct that includes failure to create a safe environment that eliminates or reduces the risk of harm. For example, if students are playing soccer without using shin guards and a student gets injured with a fractured shin, that would be considered negligence and the teacher could be held liable.

Legal and Ethical Regards to the Standards of Care

It is the responsibility of school personnel, including the teacher, to ensure that the teaching environment is safe and that standards of care procedures are in place. It is expected that teachers identify or foresee risks and take actions to eliminate or minimize those risks. Teachers should be aware of all legal liability policies, as they are expected to provide a reasonable standard of care according to their professional expertise. Lawsuits may occur if standards of care were not provided, in which negligence would have to be proven. **Malfeasance** is a type of negligence when a teacher engages in misconduct by committing an unlawful act. For instance, a teacher may give a student two negative discipline choices (corporal punishment or run a mile) after misbehaving, but because both choices can cause physical harm, emotional harm, or both, the teacher is liable. **Misfeasance** is the type of negligence where the teacher adheres to proper protocols, but implements them inappropriately (improperly spotting a student during the bench press). **Nonfeasance** is when a teacher fails to act (a.k.a. act of omission). For example, if the teacher knows how to spot a student performing the bench press but does not do so, they can be held liable if an injury occurs.

Abuse and Exploitation

Abuse is the misuse of another person or treating another person with cruelty. **Exploitation** is using someone unfairly for personal gain. It is against the law to abuse and exploit children. Examples of abuse include physical (e.g., hitting, spanking), verbal (profanity, derogatory words), mental or emotional (humiliation, sarcasm, name calling), and sexual abuse (touching students inappropriately). Physical activity should not be used as punishment (e.g., 10 push-ups for misbehaving) because doing so is considered physical abuse. If it is suspected that a student is experiencing abuse (bruises, broken bones, unexplained injuries, inappropriate contact), the teacher should make record of it and notify the school counselor or psychologist immediately. An example of exploitation would be having students do the teacher's work for free (e.g., supervising students, locker room duty).

Teacher Responsibilities in Relation to Student Rights

Other **student rights** include free speech, the right to wear certain clothing and hairstyles, speaking English as a second language (ESL), and freedom from racial, ethnic, and religious discrimination. At times, schools have policies that are discriminatory (no dreadlocks or long hair allowed, English proficiency required for entry), or illegal practices (asking for students' social media and cell phone information) that infringe on freedom of speech and expression, with the latter infringing upon privacy laws; all of these issues can cause lawsuits. Teachers have the responsibility to ensure that the environment is **safe and equitable** to meet all students' needs. For instance, a female Muslim student should be allowed to wear a head covering (hijab) at school and in physical education, since the prevention of this would be a violation of the student's religious freedom. Schools and teachers are required by law to provide assistance to students who are not proficient in English. Teachers should also not engage in racist behaviors (treating students negatively based on race or ethnicity).

Sex and Gender Discrimination Laws (Title IX)

Title IX is a federal law enacted in 1972 to end sex and gender discrimination in education and athletics, as girls had less physical education time, less equipment, and fewer sporting opportunities than boys. Prior to Title IX, physical education classes were segregated by gender. After Title IX was enacted, physical education classes became coeducational (coed) with a few exceptions. Title IX was later expanded to protect other groups, including individuals who identify as LGBTQ. Teachers need to make sure that they balance privacy and protection while also maintaining accountability and safety for themselves and other students. For instance, if the only alternative location for a student to change clothes is unsupervised, then the teacher will have to conduct a risk-benefit analysis on the steps to take.

Inclusion Laws and Guidelines for Students with Disabilities

The Individuals with Disabilities Education Act (IDEA) is a federally sanctioned law that ensures a quality educational experience for students with disabilities. Teachers should ensure that accommodations are implemented to meet the needs of students with disabilities. Disabilities can be mental, physical, or both. In physical education settings, adapted physical education (APE) focuses on students with disabilities. To make sure that the learning environment is inclusive, teachers must design instruction to serve all students. As with students without disabilities, teachers should plan intently on helping the students with disabilities to be successful or able to meet the outcomes with modifications and adaptations.

Review Video: Medical Conditions in Education
Visit mometrix.com/academy and enter code: 531058

Review Video: Development of the Individuals with Disabilities Education Act
Visit mometrix.com/academy and enter code: 100350

Privacy Laws Involving Medical and Personal Information

Privacy laws are mandated by the federal government. States can also have independent privacy laws, but they cannot deviate from the federal mandates. The Federal Education Records and Privacy Act (FERPA) indicates that any school receiving federal funding cannot share student records or any other identifiable information without consent (permission) of the student or parent of a minor. This includes individual education plans (IEPs), health and medical issues, and other personal information about the student. However, IEPs and some health issues (such as attention deficit disorder, or ADD, and attention deficit hyperactivity disorder, or ADHD), may be shared with teachers of the student to best meet the student's needs. Students also have the right to see their records or personal school files. Photos and videos of students should not be shared or posted without student or parent permission and consent. Students, however, only have moderate levels of privacy in situations where supervision is still required to ensure student safety and minimize bullying risk, such as in locker rooms.

Safety and Risk-Management

General Safety Rules and Considerations

Teachers should be competent in what they teach. Teachers can invite a visiting instructor (another PE teacher or coach) to help teach a unit where the teacher is untrained (e.g., swimming, gymnastics). Teachers should ensure that they are able to adequately supervise all students. Physical education teachers are usually required to hold first aid, CPR, and automated external defibrillation (AED) certifications. Teachers should inform students of the rules and any hazards or risks. Rules should be revisited regularly and posted in high-visibility areas (gym walls, locker rooms, high-risk areas). Dangerous areas should be roped or coned off. Lesson plans should be written to include safety guidelines in language that a substitute teacher (non-PE teacher) can understand. Students should be required to wear appropriate and safe athletic attire. Students wearing unsafe clothing (e.g., high-heeled shoes) should not engage in physical activity. Court and field surfaces should be inspected for dust and spills (slippage), glass and other sharp objects, and rocks. Ensure students have frequent breaks when engaging in moderate to vigorous activities and when exercising in the heat.

Risk Management Plans

A risk management plan is designed to prevent, minimize, or prepare for any problems (e.g., injury). Risk management plans in physical education include being trained and certified in first aid and cardiopulmonary resuscitation (CPR), eliminating hazards (e.g., sharp objects), and being aware of any medical conditions (e.g., asthma). Teachers should maintain an equipment safety checklist to identify broken equipment. Emergency phone numbers should be posted and easy to locate. Schools often have risk management flowcharts that should be reviewed and posted. Fire and intruder drills help prepare students on safe routes to take and places to go to in the event of an emergency. Safeguards should be put in place for high-risk physical activities (e.g., mats for gymnastics, additional spotters, trained personnel).

Emergency Plans

A school-wide emergency plan is often developed in advance and should be on file in writing. Furthermore, students and teachers should be aware of the basic procedures of the plan. Most emergency plans include emergency exits, routes, and phone numbers (911, principal, school and district numbers, school resource officer). The telephone numbers of parents should be easily retrievable. First aid kits and ice should be available and replenished after each use. Student health records (medical conditions, allergies) should be up-to-date. Student medications (e.g., inhaler, insulin) should be listed with administration guidelines, properly stored (some require refrigeration), and easily accessible to students in need. Teachers are usually trained in administering certain medications (e.g., EpiPen for allergies).

Protocols for Injuries in Class

In the event of an injury, the teacher should follow the emergency care plan. After an assessment of the injury, the teacher should ensure that the student is in a safe location. If the injury is minor (e.g., open cut from a student's fingernails), the teacher should administer first aid (clean the wound and put on a bandage). Gloves should be worn before touching any blood or bodily fluids, and hands should be washed both before and after treatment. If there is an illness that requires over-the-counter (OTC) medication (e.g., high temperature or fever), the student should be sent to the school nurse or other personnel, who will usually call the parents for permission to administer OTC medication. Sometimes parents give permission for students to take OTC at the beginning of the school year. For major injuries (e.g., broken limb), the teacher should make a phone call to the emergency system (e.g., 911 or school required number) and make a call to the parents. An injury report should be provided for both minor and major injuries and kept on file. The injury report should provide an accurate description of the injury; the cause, time, location, and treatment of the injury; and a list of any witnesses. The teacher should also notify the principal and school nurse of the injuries and give them a copy of the report.

Physical Dangers Associated with Physical Activities

There are inherent risks associated with physical activities. Potential risks include injuries such as overstretching the muscles, overexertion, and muscle sprains, strains, and spasms. Trips and falls due to shoe laces, equipment, and other objects may occur, which can cause cuts, scrapes, bruises, fractures, and even broken limbs. Students may also slip or fall on exercise equipment (e.g., treadmills) or get their fingers smashed by a weight room apparatus. Fingers can also get jammed when catching sports balls (e.g., basketball). Students also acquire bruises and nose bleeds after getting struck by an object or a classmate, and collisions may occur during game play. There is also a general cardiovascular risk that includes cardiac arrest. Proper supervision, however, can reduce or eliminate many of these risks.

Environmental Risks Inherent in Physical Activities

Environmental risks that are inherent when engaging in physical activities outdoors include the weather (rain, sleet, snow), the temperature (too hot, too cold), and road-related issues (gravel, slick roads). In hot environments, risks include hyperthermia (overheating), which can lead to heat exhaustion and heat stroke. It is easy to lose fluids and become dehydrated when engaging in physical activities in the heat. In cold environments, risks include hypothermia (low body temperature) and risks of frostbite. Traffic and pedestrians can also be potential hazards when engaging in physical activity outdoors, including bumping into others or getting hit by an automobile. Precipitation (rain, sleet, snow) can increase the risks of slipping, and can speed up cold-related conditions. Other risks include tripping on uneven pavement or stepping on broken glass or other debris, which can lead to physical injuries. Precautions to take against environmental risks include checking the weather forecast, wearing protective clothing appropriate for the weather, having an emergency plan, using the buddy system by never engaging in physical activity alone, finding alternative routes when visibility is low (fog) or congestion is high (too much traffic, too many people in the area), and hydrating before, during, and after activity. Teachers will need to use their judgement. For example, physical activity can occur outdoors with a small amount of precipitation (drizzle), but engaging in physical activity when lightning is present requires a safe, indoor shelter.

Liability in Physical Education

Liability is an obligation or the responsibility to perform the duties required in a job. Liability in the legal aspect is a failure to perform the duties as a result of negligence. **Negligence** is a breach of duty that increases the risk of harm. Acts of negligence that increase a teacher's liability in physical education include having students participate on broken or defective equipment, failure to cover or protect sharp objects, and failure to report an injury. Other acts of negligence include the failure to block off unsafe areas, not providing students with rest and water breaks, and failure to incorporate a warm-up. Failure to maintain first aid, CPR, and AED training is another potential liability. Failure to supervise students, to review and post safety rules, and to form an awareness of students' strengths and limitations are also potential liabilities. Teachers could also be held liable if they allow or ignore student misconduct that can lead to injury.

Disclosing Risks

Students and families should be informed that the benefits of engagement in physical activity outweigh the risks associated with physical activity. Obtaining informed consent will ensure that parents are aware of the risk. Requiring liability waivers will also provide some legal protection should an injury occur. Students should be informed of the risks through lecture, video, practical labs, or simulations. Risks and safety guidelines should be posted in the teaching and learning space (e.g., risks of weight training equipment or risks of not using a spotter) and reviewed with students regularly.

Routine Inspections of Equipment

Equipment that is not in use should be stored and secured. Routine inspections of equipment include checking for loose screws and making sure sharp or blunt edges are removed or covered with protective padding. Professional-grade equipment often used in school weight rooms and fitness centers should have scheduled maintenance in addition to the daily checks of equipment. Students should be informed of gym etiquette rules, which include wiping down equipment after use (to keep it clean and reduce germ transmission) and returning equipment to its proper location (to prevent injury). When students perform tasks such as these, the teacher should inspect to ensure safety guidelines were followed. Any broken or malfunctioning equipment should be roped off and have an "out of service" sign. The floor and field should be routinely inspected for damage, objects, glass, and uneven surfaces to minimize injury risks and liabilities.

Risk Considerations for Age, Size, Maturity, and Skill

Because students develop at different rates, the developmental stage (maturity and size) of students should inform teaching and instruction, rather than age. For instance, a boy in grade six might be six feet tall (early maturation in physical size means the boy's skeletal age is greater than chronological age), while another boy in the same class is four feet tall (late maturation, meaning his skeletal age is less than his chronological age). To minimize injury risks and liabilities, early-maturing students should be paired with other early-maturing students, as the larger and stronger student might inadvertently hurt the smaller student. In addition to the physical advantage that the early-maturing student has, the imbalance can also cause psychological harm to the less-developed student. Students should also be matched by skill and cognitive development (maturity) to minimize risks and liabilities, including safe engagement, as the four-foot-tall student might have a higher skill level and greater cognitive abilities than the six-foot-tall student, which would again be an unfair pairing and could pose psychological harm to the student with lower cognitive abilities. Equipment should also be developmentally appropriate and scaled to the sizes for diverse learners (e.g., the early-maturing student may need larger pieces of equipment).

Matching Players to Minimize Risk

Matching players based on skill level minimizes risks and liabilities. For instance, higher-skilled players tend to engage in more advanced and aggressive play because they are faster and stronger (more muscle and bone) than lower-skilled players. A mismatch in skill can lead to bullying from players with more skill or an increase in accidents as novice players may make errors that put them or others at risk for injuries. As such, the teacher could be held liable for not foreseeing potential risks of the mismatched skill levels or recognizing that students vary in skill development. For example, a novice player may be unaware of certain infractions (fouls, pushing, and the types of physical contact that are acceptable and unacceptable) that could put other players at risk.

Conflict Resolution

There are generally three types of behavior evident in conflict situations: the **cooperator** (gets along with everyone), the **appeaser** (pleaser and conflict avoider), and the **dominator** (conflict starter, bully). Bullying and fights increase the risk of harm, which increases potential liabilities, so teachers should teach and model conflict resolution strategies as a prevention measure. Strategies shown effective in conflict resolution include stopping aggressive behaviors immediately, collecting information to establish the cause of the conflict, collaborating with students on possible solutions, incorporating the solutions that the students agree on, implementing the plan, and debriefing with the students to determine the plan's effectiveness. Using these steps both teaches and empowers students to solve their own conflicts. However, if the plan does not work, the teacher can step in to modify it. This approach also helps the teacher refrain from taking sides or choosing a solution, which does not encourage students to think about their actions.

First Aid and Injury Prevention

The purpose of **first aid** is to provide immediate care to an injured person to reduce further injury or deterioration and sometimes even to prolong life or prevent death. The person administering first aid should ensure a safe environment and keep both the victim and bystanders calm. If an ambulance is required, the person in charge will have to call the authorities if they are alone, or should have someone else call if others are present. Prevention techniques for cuts and scrapes include properly tying shoelaces and removing objects to prevent tripping. Wearing long pants and sleeves can minimize the risk of scrapes during falls. Inspecting and repairing hardwood flooring and other wooden objects can reduce the risks of splinters, fractures, muscle sprains and strains, and dislocated joints. To prevent burns, hot items that are not in use should be turned off and removed from areas where students might touch them accidentally.

Modifications to Improve Safety

- **Equipment**: Cover hard objects and equipment with padding (e.g., volleyball standards and polls) to avoid painful collisions.

- **Environment**: Sweep floors before class, make sure that students have their shoelaces tied to prevent slips and falls, review and post the rules to remind students to avoid dangerous areas and to abstain from dangerous behaviors (e.g., tumbling off of the mat, tripping a classmate), have sunscreen available and encourage students to wear hats or visors when outdoors to prevent sun or heat-related conditions, have an emergency plan on file to expedite care when needed, and ensure that first aid and CPR trainings and certifications are current.
- **Activity-related**: Ensure students engage in a warm-up and cooldown to prevent muscle-related injuries, allow students to get water to prevent dehydration, allow for appropriate breaks to avoid overexertion.

RICE Procedure

RICE is a first aid treatment best used for sprains, strains, and muscle aches. RICE stands for **rest** (stop use), **ice** (wrapped in protective coating or an ice pack), **compression** (gentle pressure, usually with an elastic bandage to the injured area), and **elevation** (to move blood away from the affected area to reduce swelling). RICE reduces swelling, inflammation, and pain that could otherwise prolong healing time. **NSAIDs** are non-steroidal anti-inflammatory drugs that include pain and inflammation reducers like ibuprofen and naproxen sodium. NSAIDs are often used in conjunction with RICE to also reduce inflammation, pain, and speed up recovery time. Acetaminophen is a common over-the-counter (OTC) drug which is also used to reduce pain, but because it does not reduce inflammation, it is not an NSAID. NSAIDs and acetaminophen also reduce fever.

CPR Procedure and Emergency Response

Check, call, and care are emergency steps to take in the event that a victim is unconscious. **Check**: Shout and tap the victim's shoulder and ask if they are OK. If there is no response, the next step is to check for consciousness (check for breathing, pulse). **Call**: After this initial assessment, a call should be made to 911 that includes the symptoms. If another person is present and able, it is best to have them call 911, rather than the person attending to the victim. For example, the person checking the victim would point to a bystander and instruct them to call 911 and describe the victim's ailment to the first responders. **Care**: If the victim has a pulse but is not breathing, someone trained and certified in CPR should provide two rescue breaths to see if air goes in (e.g., chest rises) or if there is a blockage causing the victim to choke. They should then look, listen, and feel for breathing and a pulse. A protective mask is recommended to reduce transmission of any illnesses or infections. If there is still no breathing, rescue breaths should occur for two minutes before checking again. If there is no pulse, 30 CPR compressions should be administered, followed by two rescue breaths. This process should be repeated for two minutes (about five cycles) or until the victim is breathing and has pulse, until an AED or emergency care arrives, or when the person administering CPR is too tired to perform it effectively.

Chapter Quiz

Ready to see how well you retained what you just read? Scan the QR code to go directly to the chapter quiz interface for this study guide. If you're using a computer, simply visit the online resources page at **mometrix.com/resources719/mtlephysed** and click the Chapter Quizzes link.

MTLE Practice Test

Want to take this practice test in an online interactive format?
Check out the online resources page, which includes interactive practice questions and much more: **mometrix.com/resources719/mtlephysed**

1. Which of the following health benefits results from regular engagement in muscular fitness activities?

a. Increased aerobic capacity
b. Bone density loss prevention
c. Reduced risk of cardiovascular disease
d. Reduced risk of some cancers

2. Which of the following is the purpose of assessment in physical education programs?

a. To assess teacher effectiveness
b. To assess lesson plans
c. To measure learning
d. To measure objectives

3. Which of the following best describes the purpose of teaching chasing, fleeing, and dodging games?

a. To prepare students for invasion games
b. To develop effort and spatial awareness
c. To teach locomotor movements
d. To teach non-locomotor movements

4. A closeted LGBTQ student comes out in confidence to the physical education teacher. What should the teacher do with this information?

a. Contact the student's parents.
b. Contact the student's school counselor.
c. Keep quiet to maintain student trust.
d. Encourage the student to come out to peers.

5. Which of the following best describes the relationship between ability and skill for motor performance?

a. Abilities are genetic characteristics that are the same for all.
b. Abilities are learned traits that promote skill development.
c. Abilities are genetic characteristics that impact one's ability to learn a motor skill.
d. Individuals with low ability cannot improve their motor skills.

6. Which of the following safety considerations should be employed during a jumping and landing unit?

a. Feet shoulder-distance apart on the landing
b. Feet side by side on the landing
c. Soft or bent knees on the landing
d. Locked knees for a secure landing

7. Which of the following is NOT a minimum necessary feature of a school-wide emergency response plan?

a. Policies for emergency notification of parents and guardians
b. Floor plans and maps of the school
c. Establishment of communication systems
d. An on-site police officer

8. What is the purpose of using a drum to teach dance?

a. Better control of the tempo and effort
b. Provide students with creative alternatives
c. Allows students to take turns using the drum
d. Closer alignment to convey the movement concepts

9. Carlos wants to build muscle. Which of the following are general nutrient intake percentage recommendations that will support Carlos's goal?

a. 15% protein; 65% carbohydrates; 20% fats
b. 25% protein; 65% carbohydrates; 10% fats
c. 35% protein; 45% carbohydrates; 20% fats
d. 45% protein; 45% carbohydrates; 10% fats

10. Which of the following is the best reason for a self-assessment assignment?

a. To refine skills
b. To assess learning preference
c. To aid the teacher in the summative assessment
d. To practice the summative assessment

11. Which of the following activities helps students conceptualize the different levels of movement, including low, medium, and high?

a. Animal walks
b. Nature walks
c. Jumping rope
d. Tag games

12. Which activity best promotes strength in the quadriceps muscles?

a. Abductors with added weight
b. Bridges with added weight
c. Deadlifts with added weight
d. Squats with added weight

13. A healthy diet and regular engagement in physical activity help maintain a healthy body composition. Which type of physical activities have long-term calorie-burning effects after completion?

a. Cardiovascular activities
b. Stretching activities
c. Pilates activities
d. Resistance training activities

14. A male student wants to join the dance team. His parents are extremely dissatisfied and think boys should play football. What is the best strategy the teacher can use to support the student while avoiding unnecessary conflict with the parents?

a. Respectfully tell the parents they are misinformed
b. Suggest that the student participate in both
c. Discuss the risks of playing football
d. Discuss the physical benefits of dance

15. Which of the following is an effective training program to improve muscular strength?

a. Lift heavy weight, high reps, 1 day a week
b. Lift heavy weight, high reps, 2–3 days a week
c. Lift heavy weight, low reps, 2–3 days a week
d. Lift heavy weight, low reps, 1 day a week

16. Which of the following is a proactive measure to reduce risks of injuries in physical education?

a. Locating the exit doors
b. Engaging in a warm-up
c. Contacting the principal in the event of an emergency
d. Assigning students to set up and break down equipment

17. Which of the following should the teacher first consider during long-term planning of outdoor lessons?

a. Temperature
b. Playing surface
c. Supervision
d. Boundaries

18. Which of the following is NOT a commonly cited issue with fitness testing in physical education?

a. It does not increase learning.
b. Standardized fitness tests lack validity.
c. It does not lead to lifetime physical activity engagement.
d. It is often a negative experience for students.

19. Some schools and students do not have certain technologies like heart rate monitors and accelerometers to measure aerobic intensity. What alternative methods can be used to monitor aerobic exercise intensity?

a. Count steps or track distance covered
b. Talk tests or rate of perceived exertion
c. Ask a peer to monitor intensity or sweat production
d. Cardiopulmonary resuscitation or dry mouth

20. Which of the following is a health risk when endurance training in the heat?

a. Increase in heart rate
b. Increase in sweat production
c. Hyperthermia
d. Hypothermia

21. Some athletes engage in altitude training prior to endurance running events. Which of the following is a physiological benefit of altitude training?

a. A slower rate of exercise recovery
b. A decrease in blood flow
c. An increase in blood flow
d. A decrease in stress hormones

22. Which of the following exercises helps strengthen the lower back?

a. Lat pulls
b. Rear deltoid raises
c. Lateral raises
d. Deadlift

23. Students are having difficulty striking the tennis ball with the tennis racket. Which of the following will help students improve their performance?

a. Striking the ball while it is airborne
b. Using a larger ball
c. Moving closer to the net
d. Earlier preparation

24. Which of the following is the recommended range of aerobic training intensity for a beginner or someone with a low level of fitness?

a. 45–50% of the maximum heart rate
b. 50–65% of the maximum heart rate
c. 75–80% of the maximum heart rate
d. 85–90% of the maximum heart rate

25. Which of the following best describes the primary function of carbohydrates?

a. Provide energy
b. Aid in metabolism
c. Muscle tissue function
d. Prevents cell damage

26. Physical education is under attack by a powerful parent group who believe physical education is only fun and games. Which of the following laws can be used to explain to parents the impact of physical education?

a. Title IX
b. IDEA
c. SHAPE America toolkit
d. ESSA

27. Which of the following is the safest method to evaluate muscular strength?

a. One-repetition max
b. Estimated one-repetition max
c. Repeated performance of an exercise
d. Measuring the range of motion at the joint

28. A teacher notices that a student comes to school with random bruises on their body. The teacher inquires, and the student indicates that their stepfather uses his fists as a discipline method. Which of the following steps should the teacher take?

a. Contact the child's mother to verify the child's claims
b. Keep quiet to maintain trust
c. Begin the reporting process
d. Take photos of the injuries for evidence

29. Which strategy best aids in identifying a poorly executed overhand throw?

a. Compare skill performance with skill cue criteria
b. Compare skill performance with other students
c. Evaluate where the thrown object lands
d. Have the students practice without the object

30. Which category of skills best describes kicking and dribbling?

a. Locomotor
b. Non-locomotor
c. Manipulative
d. Closed skills

31. Which dance form is best reflected in the following dance sequence?

1. Do-si-do
2. Circle left
3. Allemande left
4. Swing

a. Folk dance
b. Ethnic dance
c. Square dance
d. Modern dance

32. Which of the following is a liability risk of allowing students to pick teams in physical education classes?

a. It gives students too much control.
b. It can lead to mismatching in ability or size.
c. It can lead to students only picking their friends.
d. It can lead to a poor reflection on physical education.

33. Devon has not seen improvement in his cardiovascular fitness goal of completing his mile in 10 minutes after engaging in 20 minutes of walking every other day for six weeks. Which of the following goal adjustments should he employ to improve?

a. Increase the frequency.
b. Increase the time.
c. Increase the speed.
d. Add arm movements to increase the intensity.

34. The teacher consistently provides direct verbal and demonstrative feedback to beginning students. What is the purpose of using these feedback strategies?

a. To diversify feedback delivery
b. To help students practice the desired outcome
c. To help students perfect the desired outcome
d. To help students understand the desired outcome

35. Which level is primarily responsible for the initial development of K-12 physical education standards in the United States of America?

a. National organizations
b. State education agencies
c. Physical education teachers
d. School districts

36. Which of the following is a non-locomotor movement skill?

a. Skipping
b. Bending
c. Walking
d. Galloping

37. Which of the following best illustrates the impact hearing has on learning a dance sequence?

a. The sound of music primarily serves to motivate the learner to dance.
b. The sound of music has little impact on the ability to learn a dance sequence.
c. The sound of music informs the learner when to perform the steps in a dance sequence.
d. The sound of music may confuse the learner's ability to learn a dance sequence.

38. Which type of practice is most effective for preparing athletes for the unpredictable situations encountered in team sports?

a. Variable practice
b. Massed practice
c. Distributed practice
d. Blocked practice

39. For the throwing unit, the teacher decides to teach basketball followed by team handball. Which of the following provides a rationale for this decision?

a. Offensive and defensive patterns are the same
b. Both are invasion games
c. Throwing patterns differ
d. Throwing patterns share significant overlap

40. A fifth-grade class is scheduled immediately after a first-grade class. What is the best management system to ensure a safe transition of equipment?

a. End class 10 minutes early for setup and breakdown
b. Alternate between first grade and fifth grade for equipment management
c. Train students to breakdown and set up equipment
d. Use the same equipment for both groups

41. The teacher notices that students have had difficulty getting open in both team handball and basketball. What are effective strategies for getting open?

a. Pivot and go
b. Chest pass
c. L-cut
d. Triple threat

42. A student wants to increase the strength of his chest. Which of the following best helps the student reach their goal?

a. Engages in resistance training 6-7 days a week
b. Engages in resistance training 5-6 days a week
c. Engages in resistance training 2-3 days a week
d. Engages in resistance training 3-5 days a week

43. Which of the following is a logical sequence for introducing beginning swimmers to water safety skills and basic front crawl components?

a. Floating, treading water, arm stroking, breathing, kicking
b. Arm stroking, kicking, front crawling, breathing
c. Breathing, floating, kicking, arm stroking
d. Doggie paddling, front crawling, breathing

44. Which of the following accurately describes the cardiovascular activity recommendations for elementary-aged children?

a. An accumulation of 30 minutes every day
b. 30 minutes of continuous activity every day
c. An accumulation of 60 minutes every day
d. 60 minutes of continuous activity every day

45. Which of the following best describes the recommended delivery types of student feedback in physical education?

a. Verbal, positive
b. Verbal, kinesthetic, positive
c. Verbal, visual, corrective
d. Verbal, visual, kinesthetic

46. A colleague wants to lose weight quickly and is considering taking a new popular diet pill. What can the colleague do to ensure that the product is safe and effective?

a. Purchase from a reputable health food store.
b. Sample for one week and monitor response.
c. Read user testimonials.
d. Read the ingredients list.

47. Which of the following results suggests a high level of health-related fitness for a 16-year-old female?

a. BMI = 30; VO²max = 40; push-ups = 20
b. BMI = 25; VO²max = 35; push-ups = 15
c. BMI = 20; VO²max = 40; push-ups = 20
d. BMI = 15; VO²max = 35; push-ups = 15

48. Which is the best technique for correcting a basketball free throw that is short of the rim?

a. Jump
b. Bend the knees
c. Follow through
d. Increase the arc of the ball

49. A first-year teacher has started at a school without a curriculum or lesson plans. Where should the teacher go for resources to help select developmentally appropriate activities for instruction?

a. Contact former physical education teachers
b. Consult state and national guidelines
c. Ask a veteran teacher
d. Ask the principal

50. Peter and Rob are the same age, height, and weight. Peter has a high level of cardiovascular fitness, and Rob does not engage in any physical activities. Which of the following illustrates Peter's physiological responses at rest and during aerobic exercise compared to Rob?

a. Peter will have a higher heart rate and greater stroke volume during aerobic exercise.
b. Peter will have a lower heart rate and greater stroke volume during aerobic exercise.
c. Peter will have a lower heart rate and smaller stroke volume during aerobic exercise.
d. Peter will have a higher heart rate and smaller stroke volume during aerobic exercise.

51. Ms. Paul notices that many girls never have the ball in possession long enough to develop ball-handling skills during team sports games. What strategy can provide girls with opportunities to develop ball-handling skills?

a. Stop teaching team sports activities.
b. Add a rule that girls must touch the ball at least once before scoring.
c. Practice ball-handling skills in isolation.
d. Allow girls to play amongst themselves.

52. Which of the following best describes the motor skills used in basketball, tennis, and floor hockey?

a. Manipulative skills
b. Offensive skills
c. Closed skills
d. Defensive skills

53. Mr. Jackson planned activities in great detail to ensure student learning and engagement, but it wasn't easy getting his students from one activity to the next. What should Mr. Jackson consider the next time he teaches this lesson?

a. Form student groups ahead of time.
b. Account for transition time.
c. Wait until he has the students' attention.
d. Refrain from using that lesson plan.

54. How can a physical education teacher best determine effectiveness of a physical education program?

a. Collect longitudinal data.
b. Reflect on learning activities every year.
c. Review student reflection responses over time.
d. Collect parental feedback over time.

55. Which of the following best describes the grapevine step?

a. Step touch right, step touch left, step touch right, tap
b. Step forward, step backward, step right, tap
c. Step, hop, step, tap
d. Step, cross, step, tap

56. Which of the following best describes a health effect of consuming excessive amounts of alcohol and smoking tobacco?

a. Increased risk of eating disorders
b. Increased risk of a sedentary lifestyle
c. Increased risk of heart disease
d. Increased risk of obesity

57. Which of the following best illustrates generally recommended warm-up and cooldown protocols for secondary students?

a. Ballistic warm-up and static cooldown
b. Static warm-up and dynamic cooldown
c. Dynamic warm-up and static cooldown
d. Dynamic warm-up and ballistic cooldown

58. Which of the following best illustrates positive skill transfer?

a. A proficient tennis player is increasingly likely to be a proficient volleyball player.
b. Proficiency in the tennis forehand increases the likelihood of proficiency in the racquetball forehand.
c. A player good at one sport is likely to be good at all sports.
d. Dribbling in soccer makes it easier to dribble in basketball.

59. When teaching a novice batter, the teacher should focus on which of the following?

a. Demonstrations and verbal instructions on the skills task
b. Vary distances to strike the ball
c. Opportunities for the batter to pitch the ball
d. Game-like scenarios for students to practice batting

60. A teacher is preparing for the invasion games unit in which last year's students struggled with decision-making during game play. Which instructional approach or model is most appropriate to help students with the decision-making process?

a. Sport Education Model
b. Tactical games approach
c. Direct teaching approach
d. Cooperative learning approach

61. Lisa is having difficulty balancing on one foot during her gymnastics routine. Which technique will most help Lisa increase her stability?

a. Following the teacher or a classmate
b. Keeping her core engaged during the routine
c. Practicing balancing on one foot while stationary
d. Practicing balancing on one foot in short sequences

62. Which biomechanical principle is best illustrated during the arched position of the Fosbury Flop technique used during the high jump?

a. Force
b. Torque
c. Angular momentum
d. Projectile motion

63. Why are variation and goal setting important in physical education?

a. To minimize student complaints
b. To aid in curriculum development
c. To adhere to district guidelines
d. To promote interest and engagement

64. Which of the following best describes the type of training that consists of interval training on rough or natural terrain at various and random speeds and intensities?

a. Fartlek training
b. HIIT exercises
c. Orienteering
d. Hiking

65. Which of the following has been shown to foster lifelong physical activity?

a. Competence in physical activities
b. Modeling physical activity
c. Participating in organized sports
d. Having active parents

66. During individual sports, the player does not have teammates to rely on. Which of the following attributes is generally the most important for success in individual sports?

a. Positive transfer from team sports
b. Leadership
c. Communication
d. Self-efficacy

67. The teacher is concerned that he talks too much during instruction, which reduces student engagement. Which method would best allow the teacher to systematically collect data on how much time he spends talking during instruction to decide if changes are needed?

a. Ask another PE teacher for instructional feedback
b. Ask the principal to conduct an informal observation
c. Employ an Academic Learning Time assessment
d. Have students assess instructional delivery

68. Which of the following skills is an example of striking with a long-handled implement?

a. Pickleball ground strokes
b. Tennis forehand
c. Hockey pass
d. Racquetball backhand

69. For large classes, which of the following assessments should a teacher use to assess motor skills?

a. Checklist
b. Peer assessment
c. Self-assessment
d. Video analysis of skill proficiency

70. Jumping fast and landing softly best describe which movement concepts?

a. Strong and weak
b. Strong and forceful
c. Tempo and force
d. Time and speed

71. A student is feeling anxious about an upcoming fitness test because he feels like he is going to be the slowest and weakest in his class. Which of the following types of stress best describes the anxiety the student is experiencing?

a. Eustress
b. Distress
c. Physical stress
d. Fight or flight stress

72. A student sprains her ankle in class. Which of the following is the most appropriate initial method to notify the parents or guardians?

a. Send a note home with the student.
b. Send an email.
c. Call the parent or guardian.
d. File the accident report in the student's records.

73. To improve cardiovascular health, what is the recommended amount of cardiovascular activity for children and adults?

a. 20 minutes for adults and 45 minutes for children, three days a week
b. 20 minutes for adults and 30 minutes for children, most days of the week
c. 10 minutes for adults and 20 minutes for children, three days a week
d. 30 minutes for adults and 60 minutes for children, most days of the week

74. During practice, John made all of his free throws. During the game, John missed all of his free throws. Which type of constraints likely impacted John's performance negatively?

a. Individual and functional constraints
b. Individual and environmental constraints
c. Individual and task constraints
d. Individual and biological constraints

75. Which of the following is an illustration of specific positive feedback?

a. "Good job, Angela."
b. "Angela, I like how you followed through."
c. "Angela, keep up the good execution."
d. "Angela, remember to follow through."

76. During sporting events, spectators are expected to adhere to rules. Although they are not players, why is their compliance with the rules important?

a. To keep the noise level down
b. To ensure that players hear coaches
c. To keep the environment safe
d. To practice sportsmanship

77. Which of the following is a common misconception regarding female students and weight training engagement?

a. They enjoy weight training.
b. They will have develop bulky muscles.
c. They will burn calories.
d. They will improve in muscular strength.

78. Which of the following is a benefit of progressive partner-resistance exercises?

a. The muscle being trained is less isolated.
b. They are safer on the muscle trained.
c. They have a considerably lower risk of injury than normal resistance training.
d. Equipment is not required for the muscle trained.

79. A student recovering from a knee injury has medical clearance to engage in physical education. Which of the following modifications are recommended for cardiovascular activities?

a. Excuse the student from exercises that involve jumps.
b. Allow the student to choose from a list of exercises.
c. Refrain from activities until the knee has completely healed.
d. Allow the student to assess peers in cardiovascular activities.

80. High school students are computing their target heart rates for exercise. Which method takes into account individual differences?

a. Standard method
b. 65-85% method
c. Pulse rate method
d. Karvonen method

81. The principal notices that students with disabilities are sitting on the sidelines during physical education because the teacher indicated it was too difficult to change her plans to meet all students' needs. Which of the following laws of inclusion did the teacher violate?

a. Individuals with Disabilities Education Act
b. Individualized Education Program
c. Adapted Physical Education
d. Family Educational Rights and Privacy Act

82. Choosing the appropriate skills is critical in team sports. Which teaching model is best suited for developing decision-making skills during gameplay?

a. Sport education model
b. Tactical games approach
c. Cooperative learning
d. Direct instruction

83. Which of the following exercises best trains the shoulders?

a. Lat pulls
b. Lateral deltoid raises
c. Overhead triceps extensions
d. Shrugs

84. Which of the following best describes the impact of emotional arousal on motor performance?

a. As arousal increases, performance increases unless arousal becomes too high.
b. As arousal increases, performance decreases.
c. As arousal decreases, performance increases.
d. As arousal decreases, performance decreases unless arousal becomes too low.

85. Why does the center of gravity change when the body's position goes from standing to squatting?

a. To ensure equal weight distribution
b. To reduce pressure on the ankles
c. To improve spinal posture
d. To ensure the stance is unchanged

86. Which self-assessment method has been shown to foster students' interest in improving their fitness?

a. Health-related fitness testing
b. Skill-related fitness testing
c. Comparing fitness results with peers
d. Tracking progress in journals and fitness logs

87. The English literature department has decided that Harry Potter is the book that all sixth graders will read this year. The department chair asks the PE teachers to reinforce concepts from the book in class. Which of the following approaches best describes this request?

a. Tactical approach
b. Integrated approach
c. Cooperative games approach
d. Skill themes approach

88. Which of the following best complements physical activity in maintaining a healthy body composition?

a. A vegetarian diet
b. Drinking water
c. A low-fat diet
d. A low-sodium diet

89. Which of the following best explains the purpose of using instructional models in physical education?

a. To structure activities for learning
b. To complement the standards
c. To meet all students' needs
d. To simplify planning

90. Heart disease is the number one killer in the United States. Which activities have the greatest impact on reducing heart disease risks?

a. Jogging, swimming, cycling
b. Bodyweight training
c. Circuit training
d. Anaerobic training

91. Which of the following best explains why people should always swim, hike, bike, or skate with a companion?

a. The other person can serve as a guide and provide directions.
b. Each of these activities has rules that require that a companion is present.
c. The other person can serve as motivation.
d. The other person can help in case of an emergency.

92. Which of the following best describes the impact of physical activity on the digestive and excretory systems?

a. Regulates oxygen inhalation
b. Regulates body temperature
c. Converts food to energy
d. Rids the body of waste faster

93. Jack is not following through on his overhand throw. Which feedback type would likely be the most effective for skill improvement?

a. Verbal feedback
b. Video analysis and verbal feedback
c. Written feedback
d. Verbal and written feedback

94. Bobby is unhappy that he lost his starting position and is lashing out at his replacement. What is the primary reason the coach should work on teamwork strategies?

a. Teamwork aids in achieving team goals
b. Teamwork is required for success in life
c. Teamwork teaches responsibility
d. Teamwork teaches players about their role

95. Mr. Jackson is excited to try out new teambuilding activities that he learned during the physical education professional development. Which strategy would MOST directly foster teamwork during a team-building activity?

a. Trust falls
b. Taking turns
c. Allowing students to pick teams
d. Rotating team captains

96. Blake complains of delayed onset muscle soreness after working out for the first time in three months. Which principle of fitness best describes Blake's condition?

a. Progression
b. Overload
c. Reversibility
d. Regression

97. Which of the following best illustrates the purpose of physical education?

a. To develop lifelong learners
b. To develop athletes
c. To develop healthy bodies
d. To develop movement competence

98. Which of the following safety actions should be employed before engaging in walking, jogging, or running activities?

a. Check shoes and the surface.
b. Conduct a warm-up.
c. Check partners.
d. Put on a heart rate monitor.

99. During a weight training unit, the teacher has reviewed the exercises that will be completed that day. Which of the following is the next logical safety protocol to consider before students engage in the activity?

a. Implementing static stretching
b. Having the students drink water
c. Taking attendance
d. Having the students warm up

100. Which of the following helps students build confidence to perform a skill?

a. Skill cues
b. Competitive activities
c. Watching others
d. Critical self-talk

Answer Key and Explanations

1. B: Muscular fitness activities (weight training, push-ups) help prevent bone density loss, or the point that bones become porous or have tiny holes, which increases the risk of falling and broken bones. Women are most at risk. Age is a big contributor, given the changes in hormones and lower rates of weight-bearing activities. Engaging in aerobic activities (e.g., jogging, swimming, cycling) increases aerobic capacity and reduces the risk of cardiovascular disease and some cancers.

2. C: The purpose of assessment in physical education is to measure student learning. If learning is not measured, the teacher will not know their students' level of education or what they are capable of. Teachers reflect on lesson plans to ensure that activities are working towards the objectives, thus fostering learning. Objectives are the outcomes or desired goals, but the assessment is done to measure the learning of the objectives.

3. B: Chasing, fleeing, and dodging games help develop the movement concepts of spatial awareness, relationships with self/others/equipment, and effort. These movements also help with strategies and tactics used in individual (tennis) and team sports (basketball).

4. C: The teacher should keep quiet to maintain the student's trust. It is also not the teacher's responsibility to tell students' sexualities, regardless of where they land on the sexuality continuum. Contacting the student's parents could put the student in harm's way if the parents are not accepting. Unless there is evidence of the student harming themselves, there is no need to contact the school counselor. Contacting the counselor for LGBTQ resources is appropriate; however, the student's identity should remain confidential. Only the student should be allowed to decide if or when to come out. Therefore, the teacher should refrain from encouraging the student to do so.

5. C: Abilities predominantly result from the genetic make-up of an individual, which varies among students in physical education. With practice, most individuals can improve their motor skills, but the degree of improvement is contingent upon their abilities.

6. C: Landing with soft or bent knees allows the body to absorb a fall's shock or reduce the amount of force applied to the body, thus reducing injury or the likelihood of injury. Locked knees can cause the joints to hyperextend, which increases the risk of bone and muscle injuries. The spacing of the feet is determined by the activity. For instance, the feet are close together while jumping rope but shoulder-distance apart during a jump squat.

7. D: An on-site police officer is not a requirement for school-wide emergency response plans. The other options represent minimum requirements.

8. A: Hand drums are used to easily control the tempo and effort which are then used to teach movement concepts. It is easy to strike the drum hard and soft to illustrate effort, or fast and slow to illustrate tempo variation, before moving on to music with a set tempo. The tempo of striking the drum can be dramatically slower or faster than music can provide without the technology to alter music tempo.

9. C: The Dietary Guidelines for Americans recommends a range of protein intake between 10% and 35%, although this varies according to age, gender, physical activity, fitness or body weight goals, health, and pregnancy. Higher protein intake helps maintain and build muscle. Because Carlos would like to build muscle, 35% of his diet should consist of lean protein. Normal recommendations of lean protein can aid in weight loss. However, too much protein can lead to too many calories (which are stored as fat); put additional stress on the kidneys and liver; and increase the risk of indigestion, intestinal issues, dehydration, and some cancers. An estimation that can be used to determine protein intake is to multiply 0.36 grams of protein per pound of body weight for most individuals, 0.7 to 0.8 grams per pound to maintain weight, and 1 gram of protein per pound to gain muscle. Protein sources should be lean or low in fat to avoid excessive weight gain.

10. A: Self-assessment is a self-regulation tool designed to help students evaluate skill development and refine skills. Self-assessment allows students to ascertain the quality of their own performance based on skill cues. They focus on the missed cues to refine the performance. The teacher usually administers a survey or inventory of learning preferences, which helps to plan for instruction. Self-assessment is designed for student growth and should not determine student outcomes because that is the teacher's job. The teacher also administers or determines which summative assessment will be used to establish what was learned.

11. A: Animal walks help students conceptualize the different levels because there are animals that move or travel at low levels (snakes), medium levels (dog), and high levels (giraffe). As students have often been exposed to animals via books, visits to the zoo, in class, and on TV, they tend to recognize the size and movement patterns. Tag games, jumping rope, and nature walks tend to only occur at a high level with little opportunity to change levels.

12. D: Squats with added weight promote quadriceps strength. Abductors are in the outer thigh area, and the quadriceps are in the front of the thigh. Bridges work the gluteus maximus, and deadlifts work the hamstrings and lower back.

13. D: Weight training activities are effective in maintaining a healthy body composition, including weight loss, in part because the body continues to burn calories hours later. High-intensity interval training, which consists of short bursts of very intense cardiovascular and resistance activities alternated with short rest periods, also causes the body to burn calories for several hours. In other cardiovascular activities (such as steady running), stretching, and Pilates, nearly all of the calorie-burning occurs while engaged in the activity. It is best to incorporate various exercise modalities to have the greatest long-term impact for maintaining a healthy body composition.

14. D: Informing parents of the physical benefits of dance, careers in dance, and perhaps male role models in dance may help change their perceptions (stereotypes) that boys/males do not or should not engage in dance. Discussing the risks of playing football could be a strategy, but the parents may find this offensive because they are pro-football and may see the benefits as outweighing the risks. Suggesting that the student participate in both does not necessarily support the student because he may not want to play football. Telling parents that they are wrong will likely be offensive and negatively impact the teacher-parent relationship.

15. C: Lifting heavy weight at low reps two to three days a week is an effective training program for a muscular strength goal. High reps are more beneficial for a muscular endurance goal. Strength will also increase with a high rep count, but it will take longer to build strength, as the weight needs to be lighter in order to achieve a high rep count. Muscles need rest for 24–48 hours because the process of muscle repair after a strength training workout aids in strength building. Strength training one day a week may result in minor strength gains, but it is typically not efficient enough to warrant the physiological responses needed for substantially improving muscular strength.

16. B: A proactive approach to injury reduction would be engaging in a warm-up to increase blood flow to the muscles in preparation of more strenuous work. Identifying exit doors is a proactive safety measure to use as an escape route in the event of a fire, but does not reduce the risks of injuries. Contacting the principal is a reactive measure conducted after an injury has occurred. Students setting up and breaking down equipment is a classroom management strategy.

17. A: The teacher should consider the temperature and other weather conditions during long-term planning (e.g., yearly plan conducted at the end of the school year) before scheduling outdoor activities. For example, indoor activities (basketball, volleyball) should be scheduled indoors during extreme cold or hot temperatures, and outdoor activities (soccer, Ultimate Frisbee, track and field) should be scheduled during milder temperatures.

18. B: Fitness testing is a contentious and commonly debated issue in physical education because it has been shown to be a negative experience for many students, especially if they are unfit, overweight, or obese. Fitness testing has not increased learning or lifetime physical activity engagement, and implementation is often not tied to educational outcomes. Despite these criticisms, standardized fitness tests are generally considered valid.

19. B: Talk tests or rates of perceived exertion are methods that can be used for all ages, but are especially recommended when technology is not available and for elementary-aged students because young children have difficulty taking a pulse. Intensity cannot be measured by looking at someone or someone's sweat production because these vary according to body size, fluid intake, and the number of sweat glands. Counting steps or distance only indicates the distance covered.

20. C: Hyperthermia is a significant increase in body temperature, which increases the risks of heat exhaustion, heat stroke, and death. Hypothermia is a significant decrease in the body's temperature, which can occur when training in extreme cold temperatures and can also lead to death. Physical activity engagement under normal conditions increases heart rate and sweat production. When the body loses the ability to sweat, the risk of hyperthermia increases.

21. C: Altitude training is beneficial because there is an increase in blood flow to the muscles and oxygen transport, which increases aerobic capacity and reduces fatigue; however, there are also risks, which include slower rates of exercise recovery and an increase in stress hormones (e.g., cortisol).

22. D: Deadlifts would be the best choice from the list to strengthen the lower back. Deadlifts also strengthen the hamstrings (muscles on the back of the leg). Lat pulls train the latissimus dorsi in the upper back. Rear deltoids and lateral raises are exercise for the shoulders.

23. B: Younger children have difficulty tracking objects visually, which negatively impacts hand-eye coordination. Using a larger ball increases the surface area or points of contact, which makes it easier to see and strike. Striking a ball while it is airborne is a more difficult task because it requires a faster reaction time and is a skill used for more advanced students. Moving closer to the net would be used if the student could not get the ball over the net. Early preparation ensures earlier contact rather than late, which helps with the direction of the ball.

24. B: 50–65% of the maximum heart rate is the recommend level of intensity for individuals with a low level of fitness or a beginning exerciser. Beginners need to gradually increase their intensity because working at a higher rate (70–90%) can cause early fatigue, shortness of breath, and even chest pain or cardiac arrest for those with underlying cardiovascular problems. With training consistency, the work rate percentage increases over time. Interval training has been shown effective with all fitness levels. The high-intensity movements should be brief, followed by an equal or longer rest break before returning to high intensity, as this cycling of the heart allows it to recover. Individuals with a high level of fitness can often work at 85–90% of the maximum heart rate.

25. A: Carbohydrates are the primary source of energy for the body. Proteins and lipids also provide energy, but are not as readily digestible to use actively. The Dietary Guidelines for Americans recommend that 45-65% of food intake consist of carbohydrates. Vitamins and minerals aid in metabolism and allow for cellular repair. Fats and proteins are available for energy if the body needs them, but the primary function of fats is to support cell growth and regulation of bodily functions, while the primary function of proteins is to help repair and build muscle tissue and to regulate chemical balances in the body.

26. D: ESSA, or the Every Student Succeeds Act, recognizes the value that health and physical education have on developing the whole child. Parents should also be informed that physical education is not just fun and games but a way of learning psychomotor, cognitive, affective, and social domains. Title IX is the law that guarantees equal educational and athletic access to all genders. SHAPE America's toolkit is a resource that teachers can use in their instructional planning. IDEA is the Individuals with Disabilities Education Act that guarantees a quality educational experience for students with disabilities.

27. B: The estimated or predicted one-repetition max (1-RM) is the safest method to evaluate muscular strength because it requires sub-maximal lifts, whereas the 1-RM requires a maximum lift, which increases the risk of injury. Another safe method of evaluating strength is to record the amount of weight lifted over time to see the progress. Repeated performance of an exercise is a better measure of muscular endurance, and measuring the range of motion at the joint is an assessment of flexibility.

28. C: Depending on state law, the teacher may be required to file a report personally or to a designated reporter for the school. In all cases, a person who is considered a mandatory reporter must make a report to the proper authorities any time they suspect abuse, neglect, or exploitation. Contacting the child's mother without proper training may put the mother at risk of abuse or furthering the child's abuse if the mother is complicit or a participant. Taking photos of the child is invasive and may cause further or undue trauma. As such, this is not a step that should be taken.

29. A: To identify a poorly executed overhand throw, a comparison with the critical elements or skill cue criteria should occur. A comparison with a proficient performance (e.g., elite athlete, PE teacher) is acceptable, but students may not be consistent or proficient. Where the thrown object lands only indicates distance or accuracy, not the skill of the throw. Where or how the object lands can aid in detecting errors or the amount of force applied, but skill cue comparison will help the student correctly perform the overhand throw.

30. C: Manipulative skills are a combination of locomotor (traveling) and non-locomotor (bending) movements while using equipment (ball, hockey stick or puck, balance beam). Manipulative skills involve both gross motor and fine motor movements. For instance, when kicking and dribbling in soccer, tapping with the feet engages the fine motor muscles. During the kick, often conducted while walking or running (locomotor), the knee and waist bend (non-locomotor).

31. C: Do-si-dos, circles left and right, allemandes left and right, swings, and promenades are dance moves associated with square dance, which are yelled out by a caller. Square dance is performed with four couples that make up a set where dancers may dance with another partner or with one or more groups within the set. Folk dance also has couples, but the couples tend to only dance with each other. Folk dances mark occasions like births, weddings, and other special events. Ethnic dances are associated with a group's ethnic background—some of these are folk dances while others are not. Modern dance consists of a wide variety of movements from various dance forms (ballet, jazz, hip-hop) performed to music that influences or helps create dance sequences. Modern dance is often performed in school programs and dance troupes.

32. B: A liability risk of allowing students to pick teams is a mismatch in ability or size, which can increase the risk of injury. For example, a student of large stature or who plays on the varsity soccer team may overpower or play more aggressively than the unskilled or smaller-stature student. A student who is injured in this situation can bring charges of negligence, holding the teacher or school liable. Giving students control, students picking friends, and a negative perception of physical education are also risks, but there are no liability issues in these choices.

33. C: To improve his cardiovascular fitness goal, Devon should increase the speed, as he is not engaging in enough overload for cardiovascular adaptations to occur. He needs to engage in a specific activity type (jogging/running) to achieve a faster mile time. It appears that Devon has confused the overload principle by walking longer than 10 minutes rather than increasing the intensity by moving faster with jogging or running. Devon could also engage in interval training (walk-run-walk-run), which could also help him improve his mile time.

34. D: Beginning students make lots of errors and focus heavily on skill cues, so the teacher needs to be intentional and direct with instruction to help the student understand the movements of the skill. As students begin to understand the movement as illustrated in improvement, the need for direct feedback and demonstrations are reduced.

35. A: The physical education standards are initially developed by SHAPE America, the largest national physical education organization that sets the standards for K-12 physical education and the Physical Education Teacher Education program (PETE). The state government and state-level physical education organizations adopt and can revise the national standards, which are then disseminated to the state's school districts. School districts and physical education teachers may have their own goals, but their practices must conform to the state requirements.

36. B: Unlike locomotor movements that consist of traveling from one place to another, non-locomotor movements are stationary movements that include bending, stretching, leaning, balancing, twisting, reaching, pulling, and turning.

37. C: The ability to hear aids in learning and motor performance, whereas hearing impairment impedes or can slow down learning and motor performance. In dance, the sound of music serves as a cue, as it alerts the learner when to perform each step. The ability to hear verbal cues also aids motor skill performance because it serves as a reminder of the desired outcome. Dance steps are often introduced without music, however, to help students focus on the movements.

38. A: Variable practice has shown most effective for team sports, as there is a lot of variability that occurs during game play. Variable practice provides random stimuli to help the body and mind prepare for any situation. Massed practice involves long practice sessions with little rest. Although it may build conditioning, the associated fatigue can reduce learning quality compared with distributed or variable practice, even if the practice content itself can be varied or consistent. Distributed practices are mini-practice sessions over a long period of time.

39. D: The throwing patterns in basketball and team handball share significant overlap and include the chest pass, overhead pass, bounce pass, and baseball pass. While both sports are invasion games and have similar offensive and defensive patterns, the purpose of this decision was to further work on throwing patterns in a different sporting environment. Some differences include the size of the ball, the number of players (five versus seven), and the frequency and time of dribbling.

40. C: Students should be trained to breakdown and set up equipment to speed up transition time. Ending class 10 minutes early is inappropriate because students lose instructional/learning time. Using the same equipment is likely developmentally inappropriate, given the size and strength differences between first and fifth grade, and the content taught should be different. Alternating between groups is likely to cause confusion and disrupt routines, which increases classroom management.

41. C: The L-cut is an effective strategy for getting open, which usually involves a fake/feint towards the defender prior. The triple threat and the pivot occur when a player has possession of the ball, and is used to see the available options (pass, shoot, or dribble). The chest pass involves is a passing technique and not a move to get open.

42. C: To get stronger, it is recommended to train the respective muscle or muscle group 2-3 days a week with at least 1 day of rest in between. The principle of overload would need to be implemented, which puts greater than normal demands on the muscle in order for it to respond and get stronger. Training the same muscle more than three days a week or everyday can slow down or prevent strength progress, as muscles need rest to get stronger.

43. A: Floating and treading water are commonly taught first because they help beginning swimmers build confidence, understand buoyancy, and develop basic water safety skills. Once swimmers are comfortable in the water, instructors can introduce the arm motion used in the front crawl. Breathing is often practiced after students understand the arm motion because coordinating breathing with the stroke can be challenging. Kicking may then be added as students begin combining the parts of the stroke. Although some instructors may introduce the front crawl components in a slightly different order, this sequence is logical because it moves from basic water comfort and safety skills to individual stroke components.

44. C: The Centers for Disease Control and SHAPE America recommend that elementary-aged students engage in an accumulated 60 minutes of moderate to vigorous cardiovascular activities every day. Young children fatigue faster than older children, and bouts longer than 15-20 minutes are developmentally inappropriate. Activities should include games and activities that keep students moving (e.g., tag) rather than structured exercise programs.

45. D: Recommended delivery types of feedback include verbal (tell), visual (show), and kinesthetic (do), also known as tell-show-do. The tell-show-do approach is rooted in social learning theory, which allows students to gain deeper understanding of movement concepts and competence when instructional feedback incorporates these three methods. Multiple modalities allow students to engage all of the senses, create a mental image of the movement shown, and also encourages modeling. All of these have shown to increase skill acquisition and performance, especially when learning a new skill.

46. D: Many health and nutrition products overstate or misrepresent their effectiveness (aka quackery). To combat misleading messages in weight loss products, read the ingredients list to research each ingredient using reliable sources, such as the Food and Drug Administration (FDA) or the National Institute of Health (NIH). Research any ingredients that are unrecognizable or difficult to pronounce to determine health and safety risks. Products should go through scientific study that has shown proven and safe benefits. Most dietary supplements are not approved by the FDA; therefore, efficacy has not been demonstrably and repeatedly achieved. Reputable health food stores tend to carry both quality and quackery products. User testimonials are often paid individuals or entertainers, and sampling a product that may be harmful is unwise because there may be negative effects during or after short-term use.

47. C: A healthy BMI is 18.5-24.9 kg/m^2, an excellent VO^{2}max result for teen girls is 39.0-41.9 ml/kg/min, and excellent push-up range is 18-24. BMIs between 25-29.9 are considered overweight, and 30 and above are considered obese. BMIs below 18.5 are considered underweight. BMI interpretations have limitations, where tall individuals or those with large amounts of muscle can be inaccurately classified as overweight when they are not. In these situations, percentage body fat is a better measure of body composition.

48. B: Bending the knees is the best technique for throwing a basketball with enough force to reach the rim because the bending of the knees will increase the amount of force applied on the ball. While jumping also increases the force, the shooter will have to take steps behind the free throw line to ensure that they do not step or land on the line, which is a violation. Taking steps back also puts the shooter farther away from the goal, which may increase the difficulty. If students lack the upper body strength to perform an overhand free throw, they can use the underhand technique (the "granny shot"), which allows for more force, speed, and accuracy.

49. B: The first-year teacher should consult the state- and national-level physical education guidelines. Each state has a physical education association with physical education guidelines, and SHAPE America provides national physical education guidelines, standards, and recommendations. Unless the principal was a physical education teacher, they are not a content expert. Former or veteran physical education teachers may not be abreast of current guidelines, standards, and best practices.

50. B: Regular engagement in aerobic activities aids in cardiovascular fitness. Physiological adaptations that occur include a lower heart rate both at rest and during exercise and a greater stroke volume. The heart becomes stronger as a result of cardiovascular fitness and is able to force or pump blood (stroke volume) throughout the body with less effort.

51. C: Skill isolation is appropriate when learning or developing a new skill. Practicing skills in isolation slows down the pace. As skills gradually improve, the challenge should increase, like incorporating speed, a defender, and engaging in small-sided games. While most physical education programs are co-ed, research shows that girls engage in more physical activity and are more skillful in same-gender PE programs; however, isolation of skills would still occur in same-gendered classes. A "touch" will likely not lead to proficiency in ball-handling skills because the opportunities to develop are limited.

52. A: While offensive and defensive skills are evident in basketball, tennis, and floor hockey, manipulative skills best describe the use of motor skills, which encompasses offensive and defensive movements. Manipulative skills are advanced fundamental movement skills that combine locomotor and non-locomotor skills and include fine and gross muscle movements while using equipment. Skills performed in team and dual sports are open skills, as the environment is unpredictable.

53. B: Forming students into groups ahead of time is a good strategy to save time and create balance in groups, but Mr. Jackson's problem was with transitions. Teachers sometimes forget to account for transition time, including starting and stopping procedures and methods used to get from one activity to the next. Transition time should be planned just like activities. Students learn more when they focus on instruction. Mr. Jackson should not give up on the lesson but instead reteach the lesson with transitions factored into the timeframe.

54. A: Teachers can collect longitudinal data, or data taken over a long period of time, on student progress and compare with other students over time and against physical education standards. While reflection can help improve learning activities, it is not the best evaluative tool used to determine program effectiveness. Student reflections can help establish student growth and learning, but do not determine physical education programming's effectiveness. Parental feedback can help in changes, but without expert knowledge of physical education and/or teaching, parents are not able to evaluate program effectiveness.

55. D: The grapevine consists of a side step with one foot, followed by a step behind the lead foot (cross step), followed by a side step (lead foot), then tap and repeat in the opposite direction. The grapevine is an extension of the step touch. Dance steps are broken down into shorter sequences and performed at a slower pace with a gradual or progressive increase in tempo and sequences.

56. C: Excessive alcohol consumption and smoking tobacco both increase the risk of heart disease. Living a sedentary or inactive lifestyle also increases the risk of heart disease and has been associated with similar poor health outcomes as smoking. Alcohol consists of empty calories and can contribute to the risk of excessive weight gain, leading to obesity. Eating disorders like anorexia nervosa or bulimia are psychological conditions with significant body image dissatisfaction and irrational fears of becoming overweight or obese.

57. C: A dynamic warm-up involves low-intensity aerobic activities and mobility exercises to prepare the body for the demands of more intense activities by getting blood flow to the muscles that will be used during the activity. A static cooldown helps return the body back to normal and increase flexibility by holding the stretch for longer periods of time. Static stretching is recommended for elementary-aged students because they are still learning how to move and control their bodies. Ballistic stretching or bouncing should be avoided because they increase the likelihood of overstretching or muscle tears.

58. B: The forehand motion in tennis is very similar to the forehand motion in racquetball, making a positive transfer the most likely outcome of the options listed.

59. A: Novice learners need visual and verbal instructions (skill cues) of the skills they are expected to perform. If there is too much variation in the task, the novice will miss critical elements of the pitch. For improvement and mastery, activities that the learner engages in should be directly related to the skill/task objectives and goals.

60. B: The tactical games approach (aka Teaching Games for Understanding, or TGfU) is a model designed to teach students situational awareness, or how to make decisions during game play. This approach allows for students to play the game first, then work backwards to solve problems for common situations or errors. Students develop a collection of options to choose from when confronted with certain situations. For instance, when an offensive player has the ball during an invasion game and is doubled-teamed, the player pulls from the database of effective options rather than freezing up and not knowing how to respond. The teacher tries encouraging students to problem solve rather than tell them the answers as is done during the direct teaching approach. Decisions are made in the Sport Education Model, but they are restricted to the role of the student (coach, scorekeeper, equipment manager) and not specifically to game play. Cooperative learning is embedded in the tactical games approach as students work collaboratively to make team decisions.

61. D: Lisa should practice balancing on one foot in short sequences or sections and gradually increase to the complete routine. This technique is known as chunking, which will help Lisa prepare for the dynamic movements involved in the full routine (running, jumping, landing). Practicing balancing in isolation does not provide Lisa as much opportunity to develop or engage in muscle recruitment and strength building needed to maintain balance.

62. D: When performing the Fosbury Flop, the force applied during the takeoff allows the body to elevate and project over the bar. The arched position of the body, known as the Fosbury Flop, during the jump simulates a projectile motion curve where the center of mass lies outside the body, which makes it easier to elevate and travel over the bar. Torque is a twisting force that causes the body or body parts to rotate around an axis and can generate angular momentum (e.g., a somersault).

63. D: Variation and goal setting have been shown to decrease boredom, promote engagement, and foster enjoyment in physical activities. Students complain for a variety of reasons—even students who enjoy physical activity. Districts do not generally have a lot of influence in the methods teachers use to teach the curriculum if the standards are being met.

64. A: Fartlek training is a type of interval training that is random and designed to improve running speed and endurance. Also known as speed play, Fartlek training has the runner randomly select when to increase speed or change terrain or elevation while interspersing with jogging. HIIT training is a type of interval training that has a consistent work/rest rate (e.g., 45 seconds of work, 15 seconds of rest) throughout the workout.

65. A: Competence in physical activities has shown to lead to lifelong physical activity engagement. Modeling is a strategy that can aid in learning how to perform physical activities and build confidence to attempt a movement or skill, but modeling alone has not shown to foster lifelong physical activity. Participating in organized sports can develop competence in specific sports skills, but participation does not equate to competence. Active parents can be role models, but competence needs to be developed to engage in lifelong physical activity.

66. D: Self-efficacy is the personal belief of accomplishment in motor skills and performance. As players become more competent in skill and game performance, their self-efficacy tends to increase. Because there is no one else to rely on during individual sports, athletes must be able to self-motivate and self-correct.

67. C: While having others observe and provide feedback can be beneficial to improve instruction, teachers should have effective tools that they can implement to assess their own effectiveness. The teacher should employ an Academic Learning Time in PE (ALT-PE) assessment to document the time that he talks during instruction. The teacher can conduct this during class or record the lesson and review the amount of time used talking later. It is inappropriate to ask students to assess a teacher's instructional delivery, as students are there to learn and are not qualified to make such an assessment.

68. C: Long-handled implements are designed for adult bodies. Long-handled implements also have levers (tool or a part of the body that helps push, pull, or lift an object) that are longer and further away from the body such as the end of a hockey stick or golf club, which makes these skills more difficult for children. Skills that use long-handled implements are generally taught after striking with short-handled implements (tennis, pickleball, racquetball) as these levers are shorter and closer to the body, thus making it easier to manipulate and apply force to the object.

69. A: For large classes, a checklist of skills is the fastest method to assess motor skills. This checklist can be in the format of a rubric, with particular performance activities or behaviors to look for, making the assessment efficient to quantify and look for in large groups of students. Peer and self-assessments are excellent strategies to help students gain understanding of skill performance but should not be used for the instructor's evaluation of skills because they can be objective or unreliable. Video analysis of skills is an effective strategy to assess skills, but this method is slow and time-consuming and not ideal to assess skills when there is a faster method to choose from for large class sizes.

70. C: Jumping fast and landing softly illustrate the movement concept of effort, which includes time and force. Tempo refers to the speed or timing of the movement (jumping fast), and force refers to how hard or softly the movement is performed (landing softly). Strong and weak are cues or terms used for emphasis or to describe the movement concepts, but these terms are ambiguous (e.g., the bodybuilder was strong; the illness made her weak) and do not clearly convey the movement concept of effort.

71. B: Distress is a form of stress that leads to anxiety or extreme nervousness. Eustress is positive stress and is often felt prior to a physical performance (game, dance, or music recital); however, these events can also bring on distress—usually among individuals with low competence or confidence. Physical stress can be positive (physical activity needed for positive physiological adaptations) and negative (headache, pain). Fight or flight is a stress response. Some avoid dealing with stressful situations (flight), while others persevere (fight). Allowing students several opportunities to practice fitness tests helps reduce stress and anxiety.

72. C: A phone call to the parents should be the first method to contact parents of an injury, followed by an email if available. A note should only be sent home if there is no phone number or email account; however, if the parent can be seen face-to-face (e.g., parent or guardian picks up the child from school), the message should be conveyed at that time. All injuries should be documented on an accident report and filed with the proper school authority.

73. D: The Centers for Disease Control and Prevention (CDC) and SHAPE America recommend that children engage in an accumulated 60 minutes of cardiovascular activities every day, and the CDC recommends adults engage in 30 minutes of cardiovascular activities a day or 150-300 minutes a week to prevent cardiovascular risks (hypertension, heart disease, obesity) and maintain a healthy body weight.

74. B: Given John's free throw-shooting ability, his performance was negatively impacted due to individual and environmental constraints. Individual constraints include structural constraints (e.g., height, body size, and gender) and functional constraints (cognitive and psychological issues, including arousal). Spectators, fans, and different noises occur during game play, which is a different environment than the practice environment. John is also playing against opponents instead of teammates, which is also an environmental constraint. As such, these environmental constraints are having negative impacts on John's performance.

75. B: "Angela, I like how you followed through" is an example of specific positive feedback. The student's name was used, followed by a positive comment on a specific part of the skill. Stating "good job" is vague and does not inform the student what was good about their performance. "Keep up the good execution" is also vague because there are several steps in a skill that need to executed. Reminding a student of a skill cue is corrective feedback that suggests the student is not doing this action.

76. C: Spectators need to adhere to the rules to maintain a safe environment for all involved. Rules like no food and drink near gameplay help prevent slipping; keeping a certain distance away from players and the game area help prevent tripping, and following capacity codes allows for easy and safe exit in the event of a fire or another emergency. Keeping the noise level down and practicing sportsmanship are examples of etiquette and not rules that are enforced.

77. B: Females will not significantly increase muscle mass to the extent of developing bulky muscles like males do because they have lower levels of testosterone, the male hormone responsible for increases in muscle mass. Females can get stronger by lifting heavy weights. Many females enjoy weight training, and weight training does aid in calorie burning. In general, males show more dramatic increases in visible muscle mass than females.

78. D: Progressive partner-resistance exercises (aka partner-assisted manual resistance) allows for better isolation of the muscle trained, as the partner is able to apply greater resistance or additional overload when weights are not available—a good option for PE programs that have little to no resistance training equipment. Students need to be trained prior to attempting this exercise because it is a type of training that can increase the risk of injury. Communication is critical to inform the partner when there is too much resistance applied and when more resistance is required.

79. A: The student has medical clearance to engage in physical education, which includes physical activity engagement. The teacher should provide low-impact activities that do not involve jumping, which puts additional stress on the knee joints. Allowing the student to choose from a list of exercises without jumps is appropriate, but not from a generic list or range of exercises because they may not have the knowledge of exercises that promote or impede a full recovery.

80. D: The Karvonen method for computing target heart rate (THR) zones is considered the best because it takes into account the age and resting heart rate of an individual, which is an indicator of cardiovascular fitness and more accurately estimates a person's THR. The standard method only takes age into account. Using the standard method ([220–age] × 65% and [220–age] × 85%), for example, an 18-year-old with a 68-bpm resting heart rate would have a THR of 131-172 bpm. Using the Karvonen method ([(220–age–RHR) × 65%+RHR] and [(220–age–RHR) × 85%+RHR)]), the same individual would have a THR of 155-182 bpm, which illustrates a higher range given the resting heart rate. Pulse rate methods only provide the number of heart beats, which are used to determine what the pulse is, not what pulse should be targeted. The 65-85% option is not a method but rather the range for someone's THR, regardless of the method employed. Sedentary individuals may work at 50-60% and gradually build up, while elite exercisers may work at the 90% threshold.

81. A: The teacher is violating the Individuals with Disabilities Education Act (IDEA), which guarantees students with disabilities a quality education. Students with disabilities should be engaged in the lesson and instruction given for learning. Physical education teachers should modify activities so that students with physical or mental disabilities can meet the objectives, which is Adapted Physical Education (APE). The Individualized Education Program is a legally binding plan created by a team of professionals (counselors, school psychologists) with parent and teacher input on strategies that help students succeed, like extended time on assessments, read-aloud tests, and taking notes on a computer. The Family Educational Rights and Privacy Act protects student records. Consent is required if records are disclosed.

82. B: The tactical games approach (aka Teaching Games for Understanding, or TGfU) is a student-centered model that teaches students to make decisions based on various game-like scenarios. The sport education model is also used during team sports. In the sport education model, students have different roles that include coach, player, equipment manager, scorekeeper, and other roles that are involved in team sports. The student serving as the coach makes the decisions for the players. During direct instruction, the teacher makes all of the decisions. Cooperative learning focuses on student collaboration but can impede motor skill development.

83. B: The deltoids are the muscles of the shoulders and consist of posterior, lateral, and anterior. Lateral deltoid raises best train the shoulders from the exercise options. Lat pulls train the latissimus dorsi in the upper back. Overhead triceps train the back of the upper arm, and shrugs train the trapezius muscles that are connected to the deltoids.

84. A: As arousal increases, performance increases except when arousal levels become too high or exceed the performer's optimal level of arousal. When arousal levels are too high, performance tends to decrease. Arousal levels vary among individuals, but advanced performers tend to have a higher arousal threshold than novice performers.

85. A: The center of gravity is the imaginary point where the body's weight is evenly distributed to ensure stability and balance. When standing, the center of gravity is generally around the waist, however, it moves to the pelvic region during the squat to accommodate for the lowered positioning of the body in more than one plane to prevent it from falling, thus providing more stability.

86. D: When students track progress in journals and fitness logs, they are able to control and visually see progress, which has shown to motivate students to improve fitness levels. Fitness testing can foster student interest, but many students dislike fitness testing. Fitness testing can be harmful and demotivate some students. Fitness testing alone has not shown to improve fitness, only measure it. Students should only focus on their own results and not compare them with peers because the purpose is to improve personal fitness.

87. B: The integrated model best describes this approach that includes teaching other content areas to help foster holistic understanding. Quidditch, a fictional game in the Harry Potter series, is a game that was later developed for real-life physical education based on this approach. The tactical approach is used in team sports to develop decision-making skills. The cooperative games approach allows students to make choices on solving problems collectively. The skill themes approach focuses on skill development to foster skill competence and skill transfer across games and activities.

88. C: A low-fat diet complements physical activity in maintaining a healthy weight because excess fat is stored in the body and difficult to burn. A vegetarian diet has benefits, but many vegetarian foods are high in fat, like dairy products (milk and cheese) and fried (French fries) or processed foods. A vegan diet, which eliminates all animal-based foods, including dairy and eggs, tends to be low fat, and vegans tend to have lower body fat levels than carnivores or meat-eaters. Drinking water keeps the body hydrated, rids the body of toxins, and can help facilitate a healthy body weight. Water also helps the body feel full and does not contain the extra calories in sugary drinks.

89. A: Instructional models (TGfU, Sport Ed, cooperative learning) help structure activities for learning. All of the instructional models used in PE are reflected in the national PE standards. No model or standard can meet all students' needs, but teachers can design activities and use strategies to meet the needs of diverse learners. There are formulas and techniques (e.g., bullet points, 5-step planning) that are used to simplify planning, but the models alone are not designed for simplification.

90. A: Aerobic activities including jogging, swimming, and cycling have been shown to have the greatest impact on reducing heart disease risks. Engaging regularly in these activities increases blood flow through the arteries, reduces blood pressure, and helps with maintaining a healthy body weight. Bodyweight training is a type of resistance training using the body. While bodyweight exercises can include aerobic activities (e.g., jumping jacks), results are not as impactful as jogging, swimming, and cycling unless done using a high-intensity interval training (HIIT) format. Circuit training has similar outcomes as bodyweight training and has benefits to heart health by moving from exercise to exercise, but aerobic activities are specific to training the cardiovascular system.

91. D: Swimming, hiking, biking, or skating with a companion allows someone to be present in case of an emergency. Avid swimmers can get a cramp or other injury in the water or go into cardiac arrest, which increases drowning risks. It is wise to swim at pools and beaches that have lifeguards. Runners, hikers, and skaters can sprain or break an ankle, fall, or have an accident with a motor vehicle. While wearing a helmet is recommended when biking and skating, it is not a law in many states, or there is little to no penalty for not wearing one.

92. D: Physical activity helps the digestive and excretory systems function more efficiently. The digestive system rids the body of waste, and the excretory system also rids the body of produced during physical activity. Physical activity strengthens both systems, which helps rid the body of waste faster. The hypothalamus controls thermoregulation, while cellular respiration is responsible for converting food to energy.

93. B: Video analysis has been shown to be the most effective form of feedback for skill performance, as the performer can visually see how they perform a skill. Video analysis is further enhanced when combined with verbal feedback. Performers benefit further when their performance can be viewed alongside the desired movement/skill.

94. A: When teammates get along, it is easier for them to accomplish team goals (e.g., scoring, winning). Teammates that do not get along impede team success. Strategies that help build teamwork include designing small goals that the team can accomplish together and gradually increasing these tasks. Trust activities also help foster teamwork. The coach should also communicate to players team changes and the rationale behind those changes to diffuse any animosity between players.

95. A: Teambuilding activities, including trust falls, are often incorporated before sports practice or at the beginning of a physical education course to foster teamwork. One has to depend on another to meet a goal (e.g., to not fall). Taking turns and rotating team captains can create a balance in opportunities to engage, but teamwork will not develop automatically without a common goal or objective. It is controversial when students pick their teams because low-skilled, overweight, and obese students who frequently get picked last and face embarrassment tend to develop negative feelings towards physical activity. It is recommended that teachers pick teams to balance ability and safety.

96. B: The principle of overload best explains Blake's soreness, as he exercised too hard and too fast after not engaging in a workout for three months. Blake should have engaged in progressive overload, which is the gradual increase in intensity, rather than engaging at full effort right from the start. Without knowledge of Blake's previous fitness levels, there is not enough information to determine if Blake regressed or reverted back to his fitness status three months prior.

97. D: The purpose of physical education is to develop physical literacy, which is the confidence and competence to engage in a variety of movements or physical activities along with a value and appreciation of physical activity. A healthy body can result from engaging in physical activities, but that is not the main purpose of physical education. Athletic skills can be developed in physical education, but they are byproducts of the overall purpose of physical education. The development of life-long learning is often a broad goal of education, but competence in each educational discipline is often the main purpose.

98. A: Before engaging in walking, jogging, and running activities, shoes should be checked for wear and shoelaces should be tied. The surface should be inspected for dust, dirt, cracks, trash, objects (e.g., glass), uneven surfaces, and other potential hazards. A warm-up is not always necessary for walking or jogging; they are already considered warm-up activities due to their light to moderate intensity. However, one or both can serve as a warm-up activity for running.

99. D: A dynamic warm-up should occur before engaging in weight training. The warm-up may consist of light aerobic movements or a set of the exercise with low weight at high reps to get blood flow to the desired muscles. Static stretching or holding a stretch pools blood to one area rather than the entire body and is recommended to be done at the end of a workout to increase flexibility. Attendance can be taken while students warm up to save time and increase activity time. Not all students will need water prior to weight training workout, but they may need water after the warm-up and during the workout.

100. C: Watching other classmates perform a skill helps students build confidence. Skill cues help with the understanding of how to perform a skill but do not build confidence independently. Many students are not competitive, and competition has shown to hinder confidence for novice learners. Positive self-talk may help build confidence, but negative or overly critical self-talk hinders confidence and skill performance.

Online Resources

Due to our efforts to try to keep this book to a manageable length, we've created a link that will give you access to all of your online resources:

mometrix.com/resources719/mtlephysed

It's Your Moment, Let's Celebrate It!

Share your story @mometrixtestpreparation